MW01130732

MASTER CLASS

The Complete Guide to Understanding and Applying Chord Structures on the Bass Guitar

**by
Dominik Hauser**

Speed • Pitch • Balance • Loop

To access audio visit:
www.halleonard.com/mylibrary

Enter Code
2743-3585-9122-7038

ISBN: 978-1-4234-1198-7

7777 W. BLUEMOUND RD. P.O. BOX 13819 MILWAUKEE, WI 53213

In Australia Contact:
Hal Leonard Australia Pty. Ltd.
4 Lentara Court
Cheltenham, Victoria, 3192 Australia
Email: ausadmin@halleonard.com

Visit Hal Leonard Online at
www.halleonard.com

Dedication and Acknowledgments

I would like to dedicate this book to my wife Nancy. Thank you for your unending support and love.

Bass—Dominik Hauser
Guitars—Kevin Tiernan
Drums, Percussion, and HandSonic®—Kurt Walther
Keyboard, Drums, and String Programming—Dominik Hauser
Mixing Engineer—Mike Aarvold

Thanks to Barrett Tagliarino for reviewing my manuscript, Kevin and Kurt for their amazing performances, and Mike for the great mix.

About the Author

Born in Switzerland, Dominik Hauser was educated at Jazz School St. Gallen where he received his master's degree in music. As composer, arranger, and bass player for the jazz-funk group the Ruleless he was awarded the prestigious Prix Walo and performed at the Montreux Jazz Festival. After moving to Los Angeles in 1996 he studied film scoring at UCLA and began working in the industry composing for independent films. Dominik is a sought-after bass instructor at the Musicians Institute, where he teaches arranging in the MI degree program, along with jazz studies, fretboard improvisation, and computer notation. He also plays sessions and gigs in the L.A. studio and club scene. Listen to some of Dominik's compositions and find out about his latest projects at hausermusic.com.

Contents

		Page	Track
Introduction		4	
	About the Audio	4	
	Equipment	4	
1.	**How to Play Chords on Bass**	5	
2.	**Double Stops**	6	1–8
	Single Interval Exercises	10	9–17
	Combined Interval Exercises	15	
	"Jingle Bells"	15	18
	"Lullaby"	17	19
	"Peter and the Wolf"	18	20
	"Toreador, en Garde"	18	21
	"Song for My Mother"	19	22
3.	**Major Triads**	20	
	Triad Studies in C—Closed Voicings	21	23–24
	"Ode to Joy" (in C)	22	25
	Triad Studies in B♭—Open Voicings	24	26–27
	"Ode to Joy" (in B♭)	25	28
4.	**Minor Triads**	26	
	Triad Studies in Cmi—Closed Voicings	27	29–30
	"Bouree" (in B♭mi)	28	31
	Triad Studies in Cmi—Open Voicings	30	32–33
	"Bouree" (in Cmi)	31	34
5.	**Diminished and Augmented Triads**	32	
6.	**Mixed Triad Exercises**	34	35–44
	Montuno Pattern	41	45
	"Greensleeves"	42	46
	"Amazing Grace"	44	47
7.	**Seventh Chords**	45	
8.	**Seventh Chord Exercises**	51	
	Chord Progression in C	51	48
	Chord Progression in B♭	51	49
	Arpeggiated Chord Progression in G	52	50
	Broken Chord Progression in F	52	51
	Jazz Blues in F	53	52
	"When the Saints Go Marching In"	54	53
	"Go Tell It on the Mountain"	54	54
	"Looking Back"	56	55
9.	**Playing Chords with a Bass Line**	58	
	I–IV–I–IV–V in C	58	56
	I–IV–I–II–V in D	58	57
	II–V–I in C	59	58–59
	II–V–I–IV in B♭	59	60–61
	Rock Groove in Fmi	60	62
	Gospel Groove in G	60	63
	Walking Bass Line with 3rd and 7th Chord Fragments	60	64–66
	Funk Rock Pattern with Passing Chords	62	67
	Funk Rock Patterns over B♭ Blues Progression	62	68
10.	**Using Chords in Different Styles**	63	
	Heavy Metal	63	69
	Grunge	64	70
	Funk	65	71
	Funk Rock	66	72
	Jazz	67	73–74
	Bossa Nova	69	75
	Rock 'n' Roll	70	76
11.	**Chord Glossary**	71	
	Triads	71	
	Sixth Chords	72	
	Seventh Chords	73	
	Extended Chords	76	
	Altered Chords	79	

Introduction

Welcome to *Chords for Bass*. This is an exciting opportunity to explore fresh new sounds in your bass playing you may have never considered. Learning to play chords will also help you find more interesting notes when playing bass lines in the regular way. It will enhance your ability to hear chord progressions and chord qualities, and to compose and arrange songs, as well as improving your soloing chops and overall musicianship.

Usually chords are covered only briefly in bass method books or just in the context of specific licks. This is the first book to present a complete method for understanding and applying all the practical possibilities for chords the instrument has to offer.

Accomplished bass players in the past (notably Stanley Clarke and Jaco Pastorius) used some chords, but mostly limited themselves to only two notes at a time. A good example of a modern bassist who exploits the chordal possibilities of the bass to their fullest extent is Michael Manring.

I've found in my career as a bass player that chords are useful in many situations, especially in trio settings with a guitarist or when no one else is playing chords. Doubling chords in rock situations can be very powerful, and spicing up a funk bass line with chord fills is a welcome novelty.

As a teacher I find it adds a lot of clarity to play chords behind my students as they play exercises, to provide them with the harmonic background. Teaching the students chords helps them understand how other musicians—especially pianists and guitarists—think about the music.

The chords in this book are mostly two- or three-note versions (known as *voicings*) but we'll learn about how to imply chords that may contain as many as four or five notes. We are forced to do this because of the technical limitations and low sonic range of the bass. All the examples in the book are geared toward helping you use chords that sound good in a band situation. They're written for the four-string bass so that everyone can play them. They can be adapted by five- and six-string players, but keep in mind that having lower strings on the bass is not really going to add to the available chord voicings—they're too muddy down there! An added high string (usually on the six-string bass) gives you many more chord possibilities.

Most of the examples include chord symbols. The actual bass part is an interpretation of those chords that you can try to apply to similar chords or progressions. As any decent guitarist or pianist will tell you, it is not always necessary to play all the notes of a written chord. The chord symbol is a framework from whence you start building your part.

About the Audio

Listen closely to not only the bass parts as they are played on the accompanying audio tracks, but also to the way the other instruments—drums, guitars, and keyboards—are arranged. In a band situation, it's important to make sure that everyone cooperates in not stepping on each other's parts. Since you're playing chords on your bass, you're not in a register that you usually use, so the other instrumentalists may accommodate you by playing sparser or higher parts, or they may take over your usual role and hold down the bass line. The bass is panned to the right channel on the audio tracks. If you would like to listen only to the bass, pan your stereo to that side. If you would like to play along with the track without the bass, pan to the left and you will hear drums, guitars, and keyboards.

Equipment

Any fretted bass and any amplifier are usually well-suited for playing chords. The main thing to look out for is keeping clarity in the sound. Because you're playing multiple notes in a low range, it's best to dial out some of the low frequencies to avoid muddiness. You can add a little high end, but it's more important to take out some lows. A balanced tone will let you switch between chords and single-note playing without changing settings. A low string action on your bass can make it a little easier to play chords, but the way you have your bass set up for normal playing should be fine.

I recommend not trying to play chords on the fretless bass at all; it's very difficult to keep the notes in tune.

1 How to Play Chords on Bass

Most of the time we'll be playing on the top two or possibly three strings. It is necessary to keep some arch in the fret-hand fingers so that higher notes are not accidentally damped by the fingers that are playing the lower ones. Unused fingers and the lower parts of the fingers, or the fingertips in some cases, can be used to prevent unwanted open strings from vibrating.

In the picking hand, use your index and middle fingers to play any adjacent two strings of the bass. Most often you'll be playing the top two strings like this. If there is a third, lower note on either the A or E string, use your thumb to play it. This style is most adaptable for incorporating with regular two-fingered bass playing.

Double stops are any two notes played at the same time. You'll use your right-hand index finger for the low note and the middle finger for the high note in the example below.

To pluck three-note chords, use your thumb for the lowest note, the index for the middle note, and the middle finger for the high note. We'll talk more about the theory of chord construction in later chapters. Right now we're just discussing technique.

For four-note chords, we use the same fingers as before, only now the highest note is played by the right-hand ring finger. Chord voicings like this are very thick-sounding, so we tend not to use them very much.

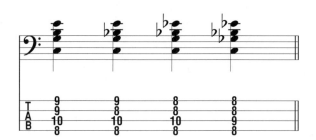

Double Stops

2

All chords are derived from a scale. The most common scale is the *major* or Ionian scale, shown here in the key of C. The major scale is used to describe all other musical concepts that follow, like intervals, triads, and seventh chords.

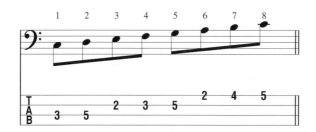

The notes of the scale have the letter names that you probably already know (C–D–E–F–G–A–B–C), but more importantly, they're referred to as *scale degrees*, with the numbers 1–2–3–4–5–6–7–8. Notes and chords that belong to one scale are said to be *diatonic*.

If you play notes 1 and 3 together (C and E), you will get a double stop called a *3rd*. This is an *interval*.

For each note in the major scale there is an interval with the same name: 2nd, 3rd, 4th, etc., that is measured from the *root* (the starting note, in this case, C) to the higher note. The 8th interval is called an *octave*.

The most commonly-played intervals on the bass are 3rds, 4ths, 5ths, and 6ths. The 3rds and 6ths sound the prettiest. 2nds and 7ths are omitted in these examples because they don't sound good by themselves.

3rds and 6ths may be major or *minor*. In a minor interval, the high note is lowered by one fret.

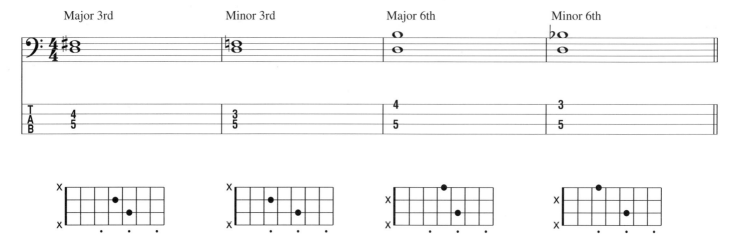

6

If you invert a major 3rd you get a minor 6th.   If you invert a minor 3rd you get a major 6th.

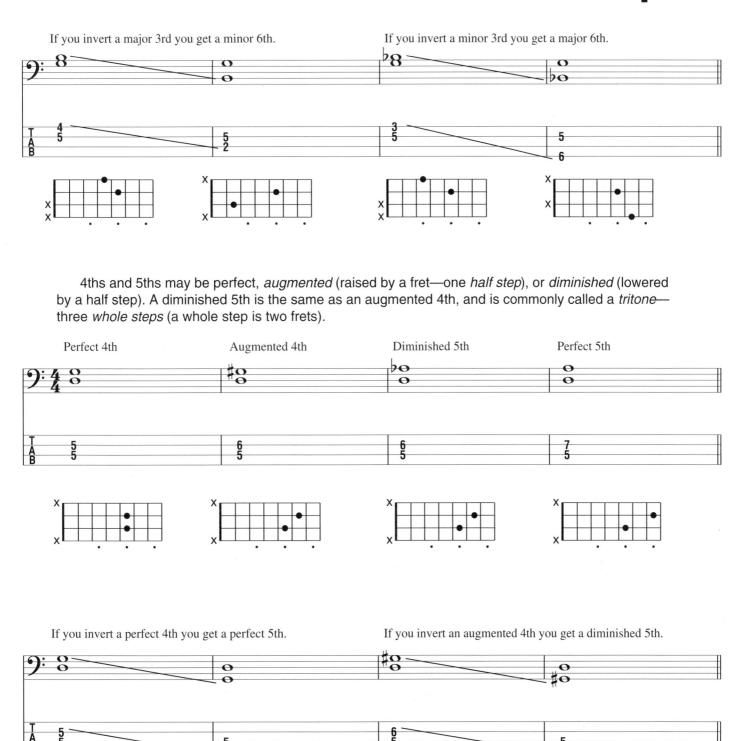

4ths and 5ths may be perfect, *augmented* (raised by a fret—one *half step*), or *diminished* (lowered by a half step). A diminished 5th is the same as an augmented 4th, and is commonly called a *tritone*—three *whole steps* (a whole step is two frets).

Perfect 4th   Augmented 4th   Diminished 5th   Perfect 5th

If you invert a perfect 4th you get a perfect 5th.   If you invert an augmented 4th you get a diminished 5th.

On the audio, diatonic 3rds, 6ths, 4ths, and 5ths are played in a few keys to give you the idea, but you should practice in all twelve possible keys.

F Major Scale in Diatonic 3rds, Harmony in Top Voice

Track 1

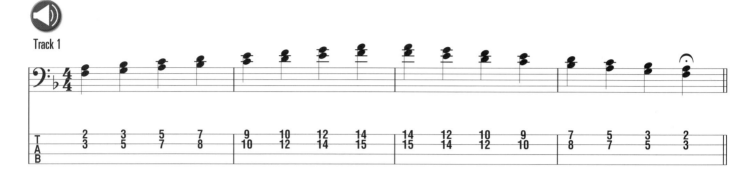

F Major Scale in Diatonic 3rds, Harmony in Bottom Voice

Track 2

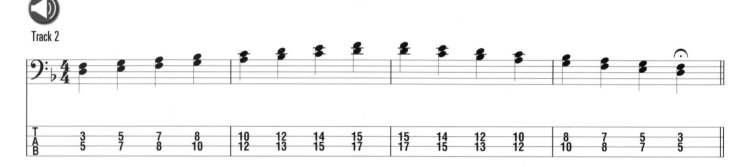

C Major Scale in Diatonic 6ths, Harmony in Top Voice

Track 3

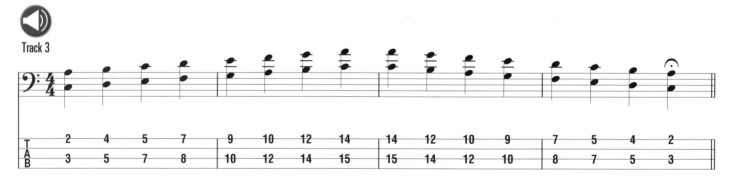

C Major Scale in Diatonic 6ths, Harmony in Bottom Voice

Track 4

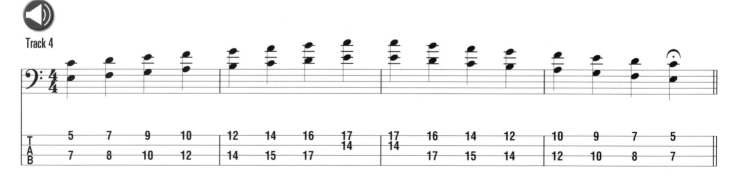

G Major Scale in Diatonic 4ths, Harmony in Top Voice

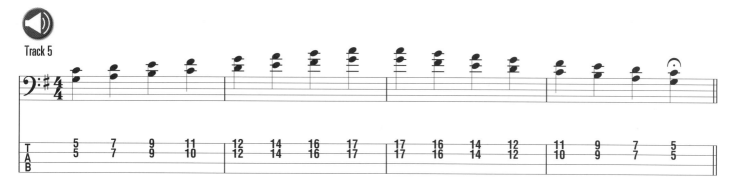

Track 5

G Major Scale in Diatonic 4ths, Harmony in Bottom Voice

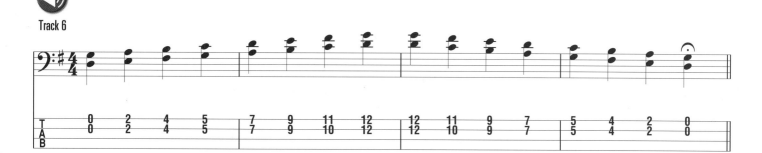

Track 6

E♭ Major Scale in Diatonic 5ths, Harmony in Top Voice

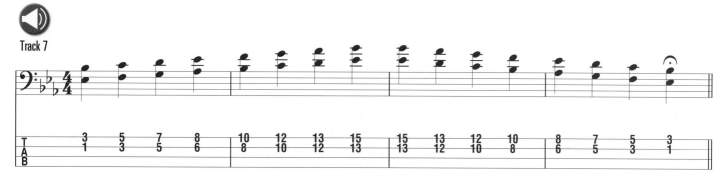

Track 7

B♭ Major Scale in Diatonic 5ths, Harmony in Bottom Voice

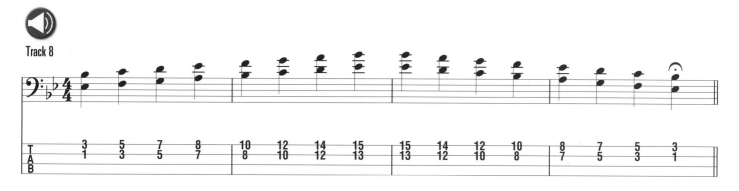

Track 8

Single Interval Exercises

Now that we've seen, heard, and played the common intervals up and down the scale, we still need practice. Here are some exercises. Each uses only one kind of interval.

By only using 3rds the first two examples have a classical flavor.

Track 9

Track 10

We get a funkier feel by using sixteenth-note rhythms that are *syncopated*. A syncopated note or chord is one that is not played on the strong beats—1, 2, 3, or 4—but on one of the smaller subdivisions of time before or after. Notice in this example how the guitar plays high voicings so it doesn't clash with the bass chords.

Track 11

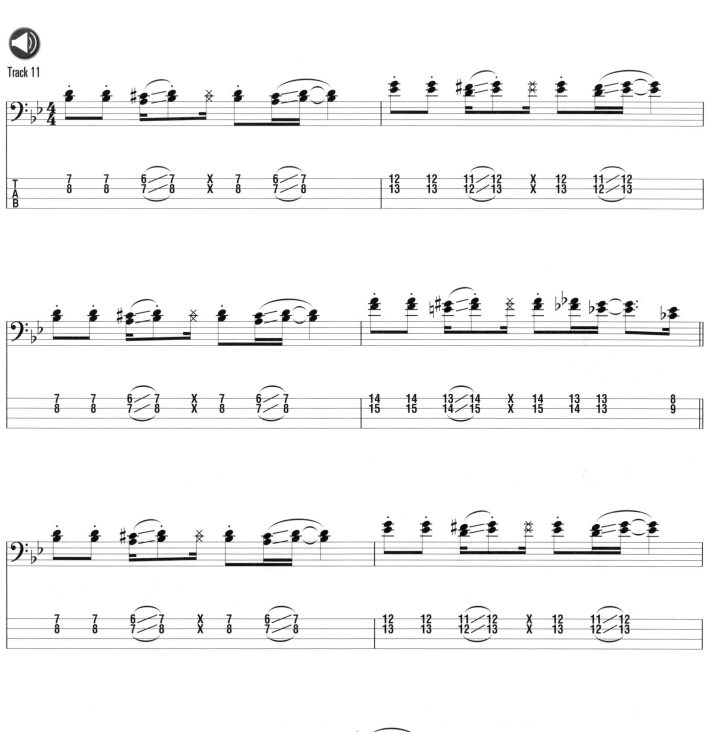

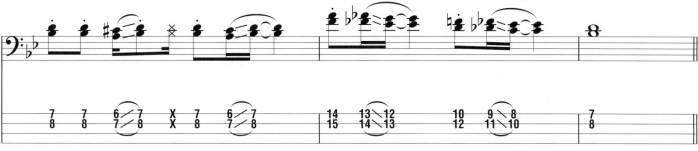

Here are some examples with 6ths. The first one has a classical feel.

Track 12

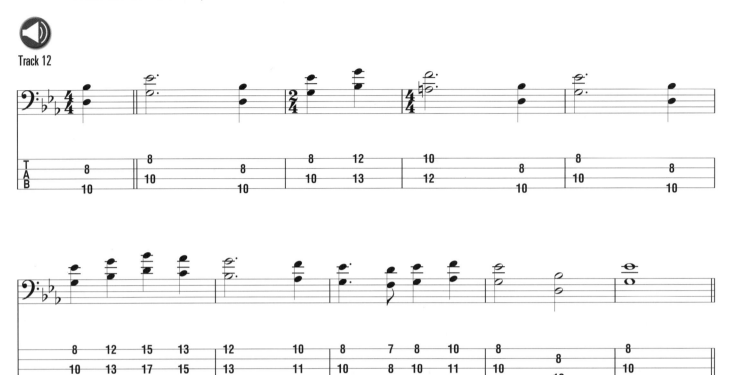

Adding more *chromatic* (one-fret) moves and inverting the chords gives a progressive rock sound. Here the guitar plays a melody, leaving room for the bass chords.

Track 13

let ring - - - - - ⌐

4ths are great for blues and rock. The following two examples are in C minor. Here the guitar doubles the bass on the main accents. Between these accents the guitar plays ghost notes to propel the groove.

Track 14

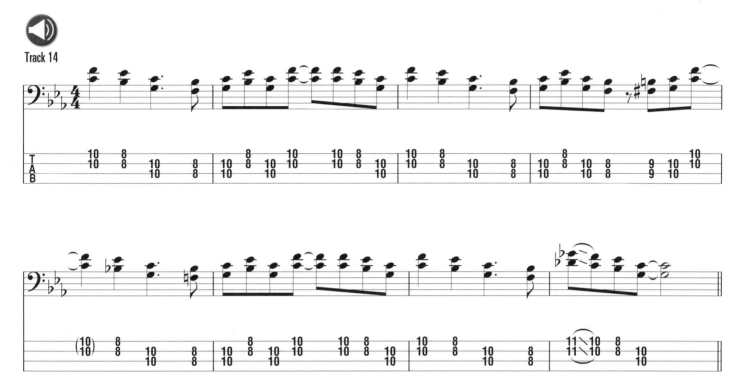

Here the guitar plays a sparse melody, again leaving room for the bass chords.

Track 15

5ths are the preferred instrument of destruction by metalheads. Try them with and without distortion. The guitar plays harmony notes, matching the rhythm of the bass.

Track 16

Here the guitar doubles the bass on the main accents, and plays ghost notes to drive the rhythm forward.

Track 17

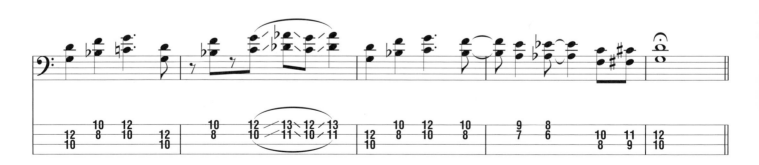

Combined Interval Exercises

Now let's learn some familiar tunes arranged with double stops. They use parts of chord shapes that we'll study in further depth as we go along. For now, focus on playing these little songs with clean technique, with no extra open strings ringing out. Some require stretches that will take time to get used to. Don't rush it.

"Jingle Bells"

by J. Pierpont

The acoustic guitar fills in the harmonies with high voicings.

Track 18

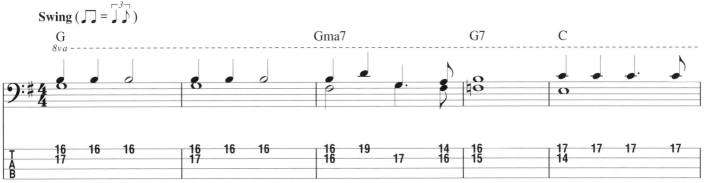

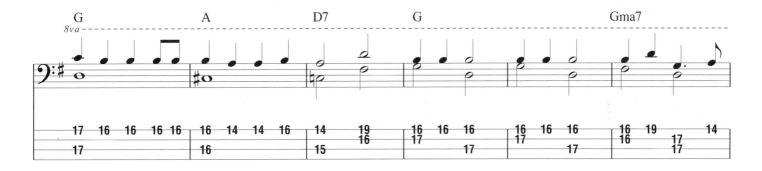

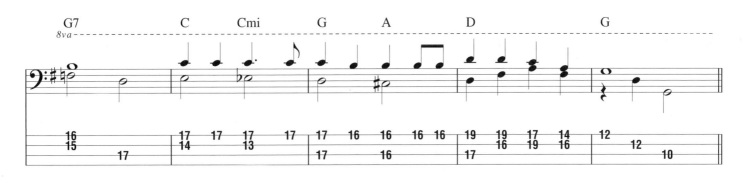

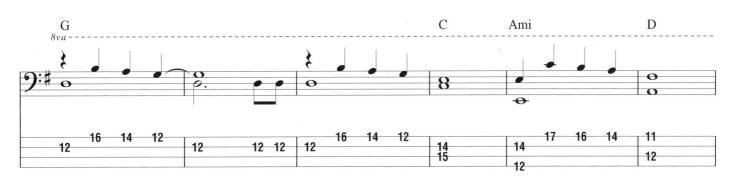

"Lullaby"
by Johannes Brahms

On this track the strings reinforce the partial harmonies of the bass.

Track 19

"Peter and the Wolf"
by Sergei Prokofiev

Here the strings reinforce the partial harmonies of the bass and create a sense of motion by playing the upbeats.

Track 20

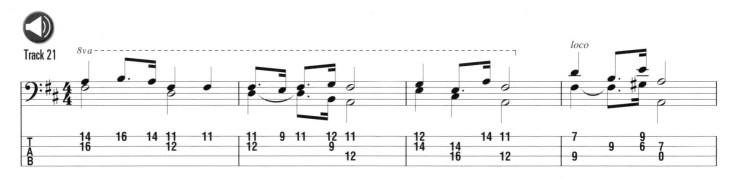

"Toreador, en Garde"
by Georges Bizet

Track 21

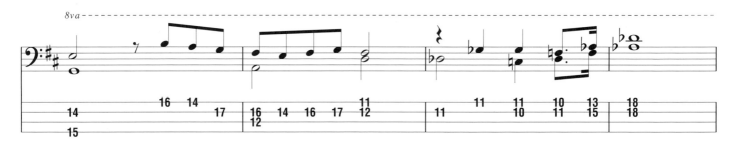

"Song for My Mother"
by Dominik Hauser

Major Triads

3

The major triad can be derived by taking the root, 3rd, and 5th degrees of the major scale.

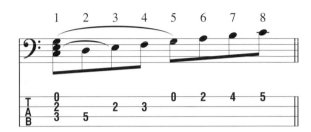

A chord is *inverted* when its lowest note is not the root. Here is a C major triad in *root position* and the two possible inversions.

I Chord

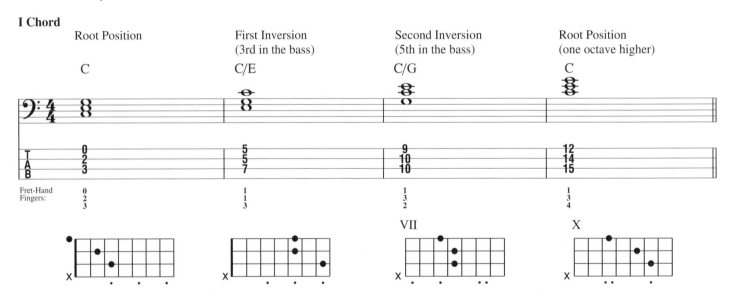

Many simple songs use only three major triads that are derived from the same major scale (in other words, they are diatonic chords). They are called the I, IV, and V ("one," "four," and "five") chords. In the key of C, the IV chord is F major.

IV Chord

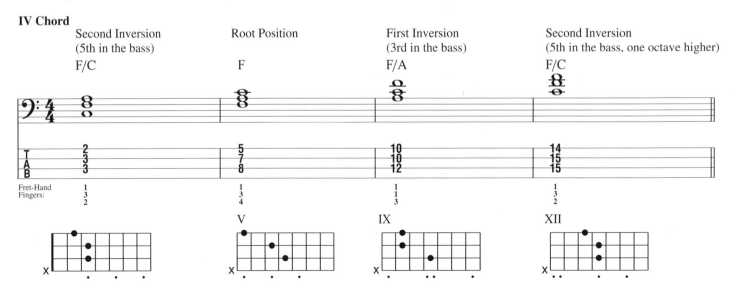

The V chord in C is G major.

V Chord

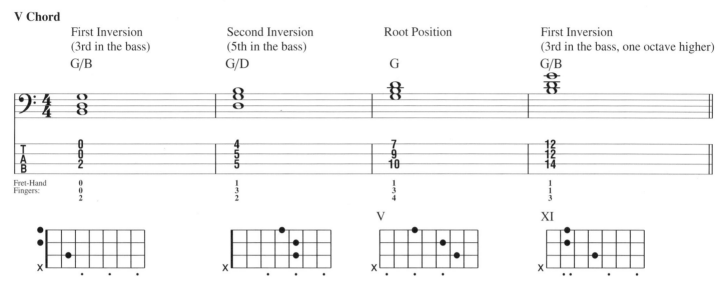

These chords are *closed* voicings; that is, the notes are as close together as possible.

Triad Studies in C—Closed Voicings

Track 23

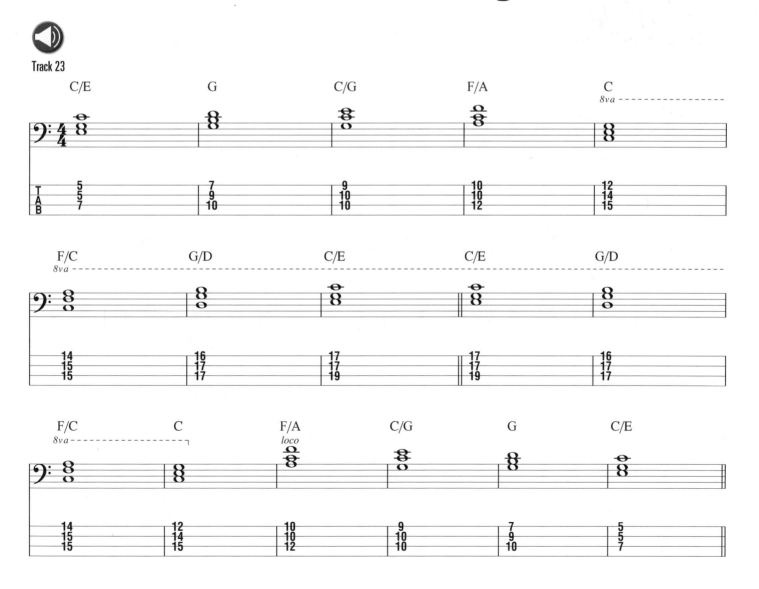

Having the guitar play sparse chords adds to the texture of this exercise.

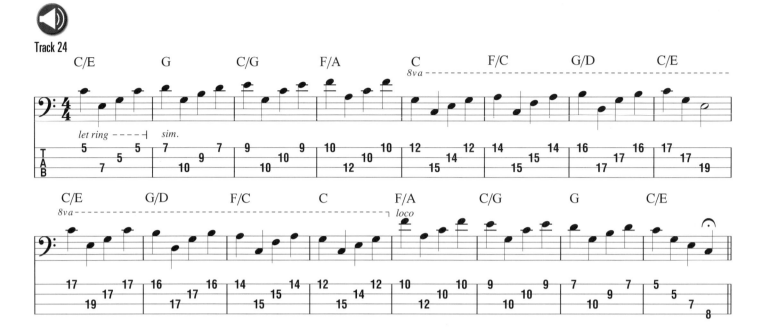

Track 24

"Ode to Joy" (in C)

by Ludwig van Beethoven

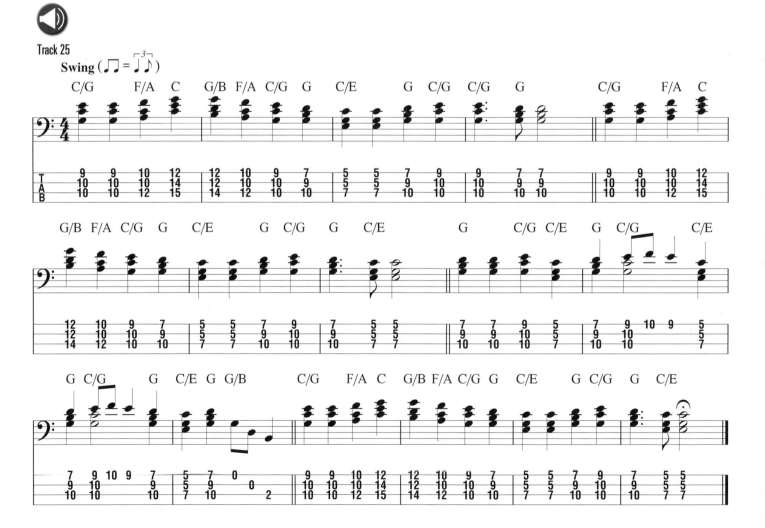

Track 25

These next examples are in the key of B♭ and are *open* voicings, created by raising the middle note by an octave.

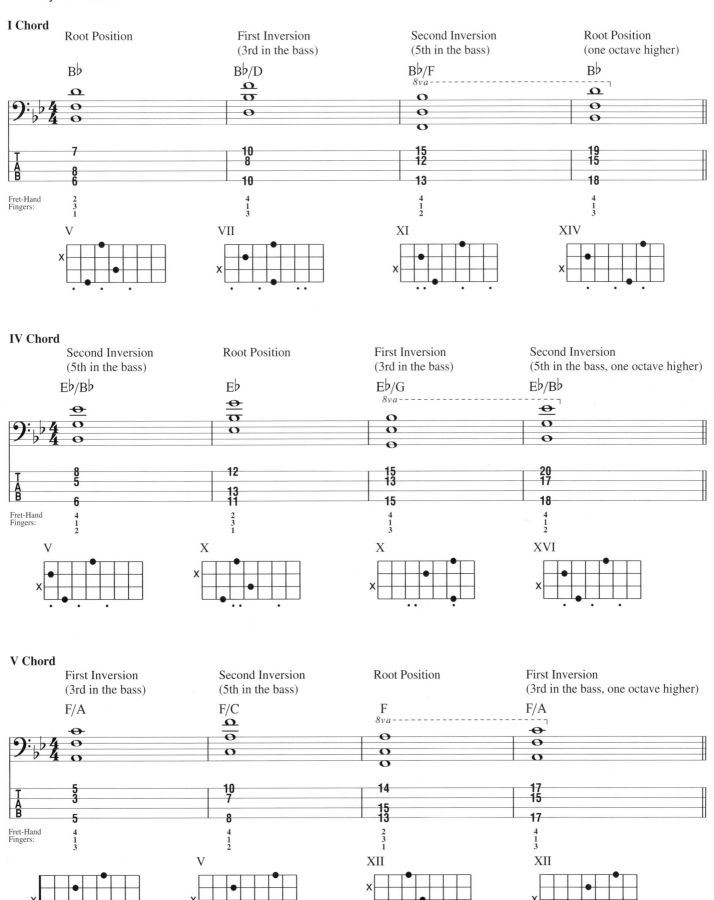

I Chord

| Root Position | First Inversion (3rd in the bass) | Second Inversion (5th in the bass) | Root Position (one octave higher) |

IV Chord

| Second Inversion (5th in the bass) | Root Position | First Inversion (3rd in the bass) | Second Inversion (5th in the bass, one octave higher) |

V Chord

| First Inversion (3rd in the bass) | Second Inversion (5th in the bass) | Root Position | First Inversion (3rd in the bass, one octave higher) |

Triad Studies in B♭—Open Voicings

Having the guitar arpeggiate the chords complements the rhythm of the bass.

"Ode to Joy" (in B♭)
by Ludwig van Beethoven

Track 28 Swing (♫ = ♩♪)

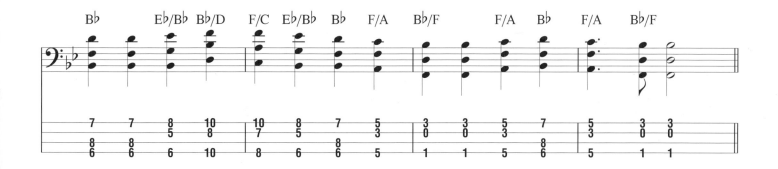

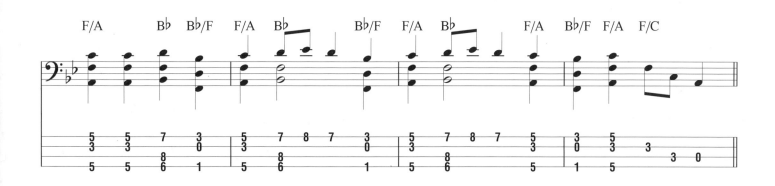

Minor Triads

In a minor key, the I, IV, and V chords are minor in quality. Here are the three different fingerings for the minor triads in closed position in the key of C minor.

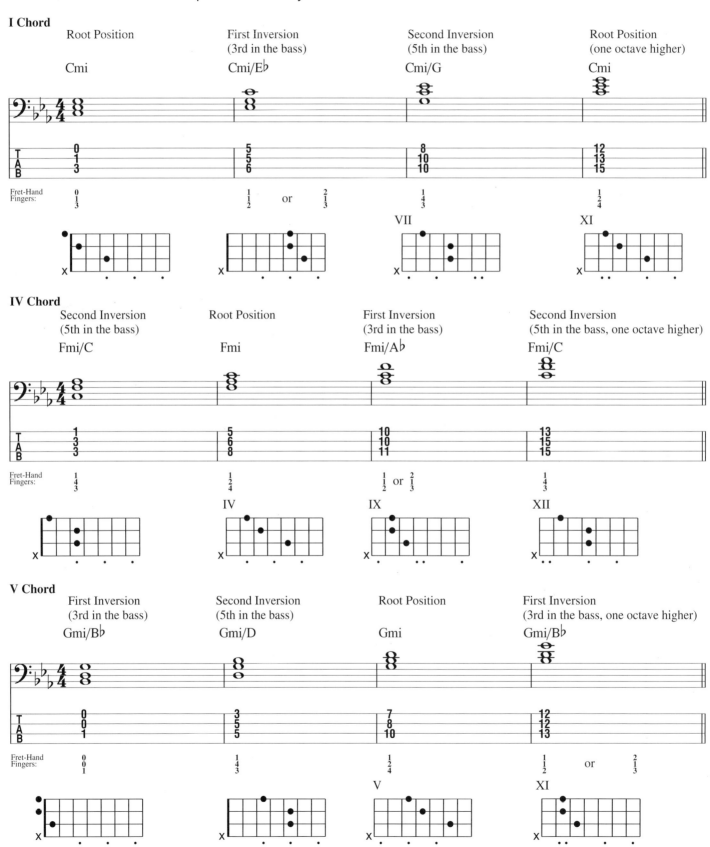

Triad Studies in Cmi—Closed Voicings

These bass chords support a faint piano melody.

Track 29

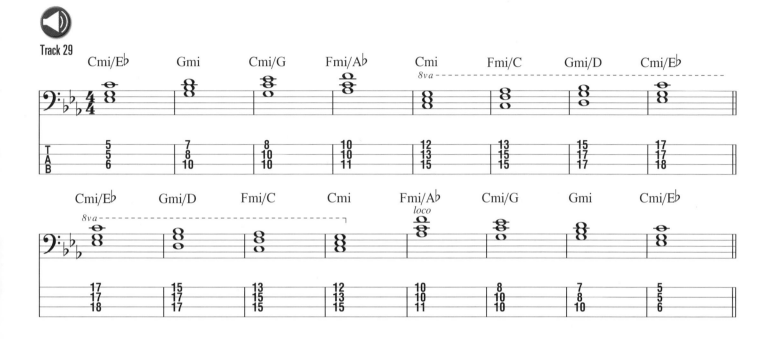

The strings create a pad that the bass can play against.

Track 30

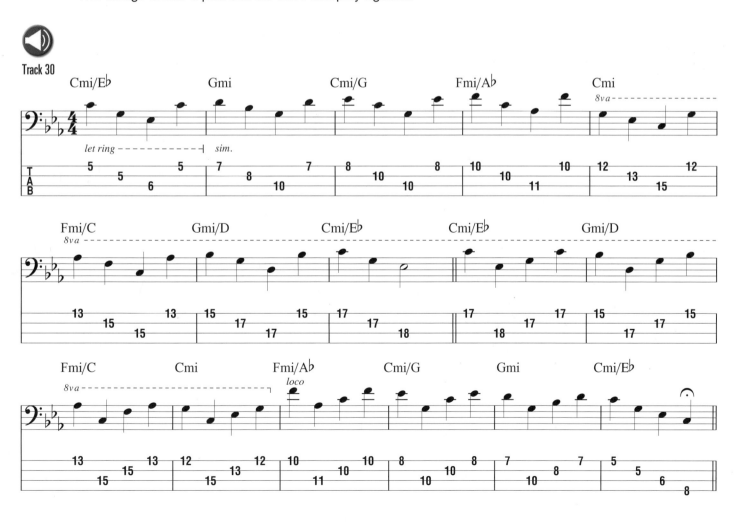

"Bouree" (in B♭mi)

by J. S. Bach

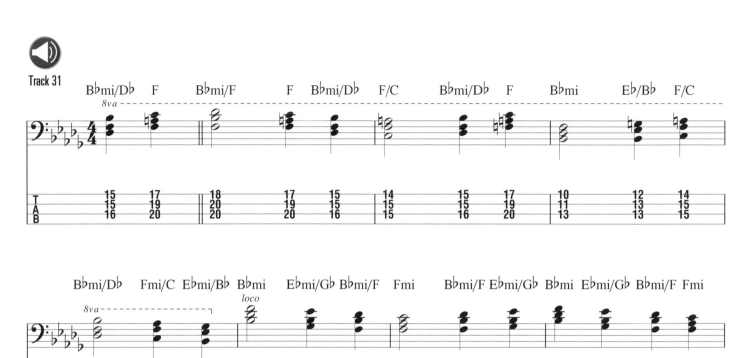

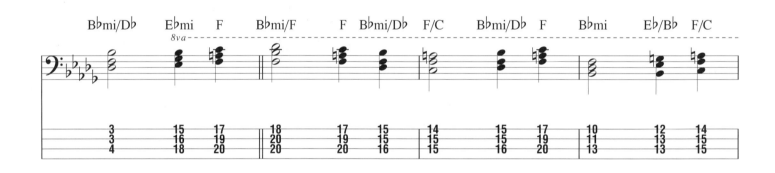

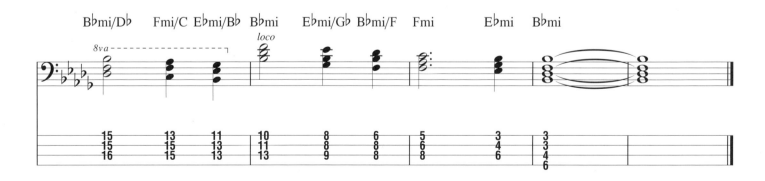

Here we have open voicings for the I, IV, and V chords in the key of C minor.

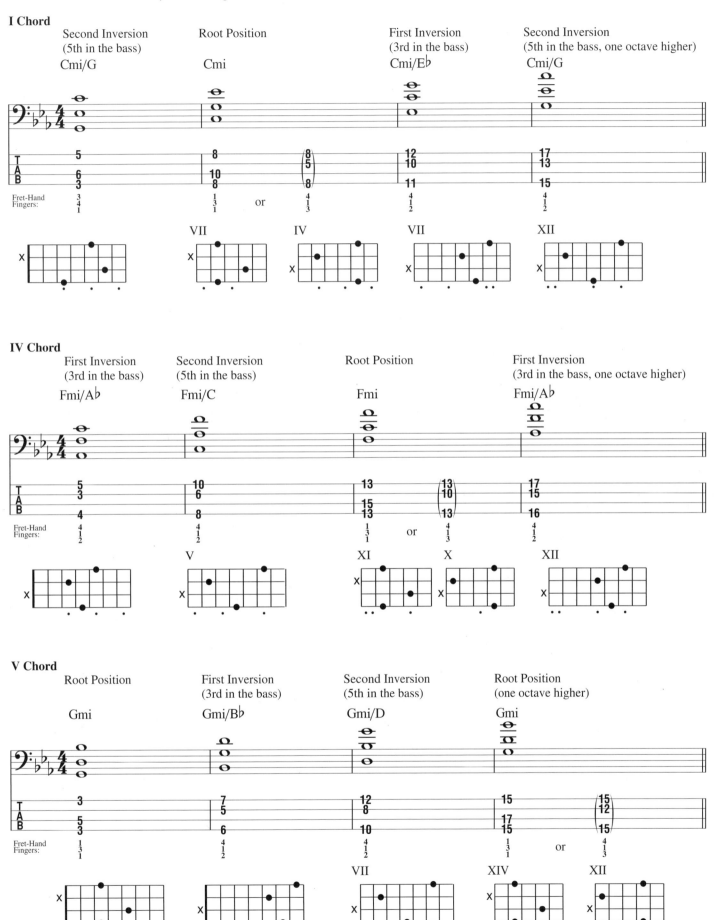

4

Triad Studies in Cmi—Open Voicings

A faint synth melody supported by bass chords.

30

"Bouree" (in Cmi)
by J. S. Bach

Track 34

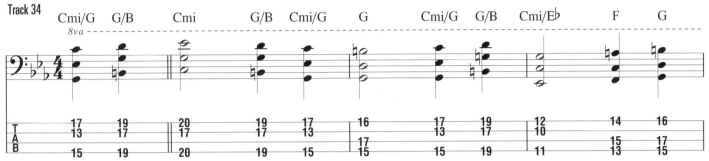

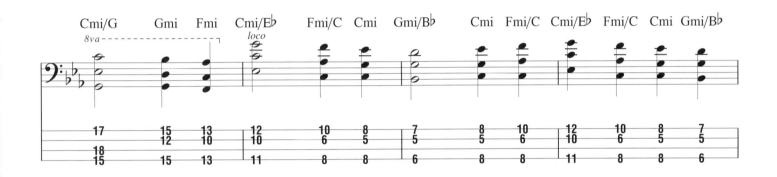

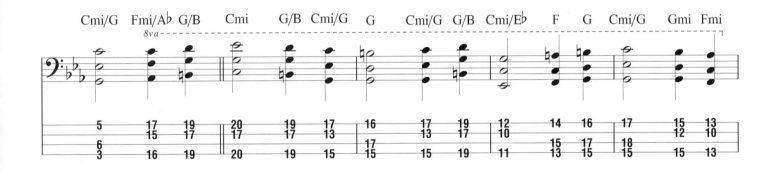

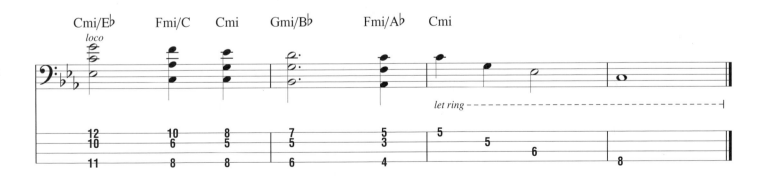

5 Diminished and Augmented Triads

A diminished triad consists of two minor 3rds stacked one on top of the other. The VII triad in diatonic major harmony is diminished. Here are the three different fingerings for the diminished triad in **closed** voicings.

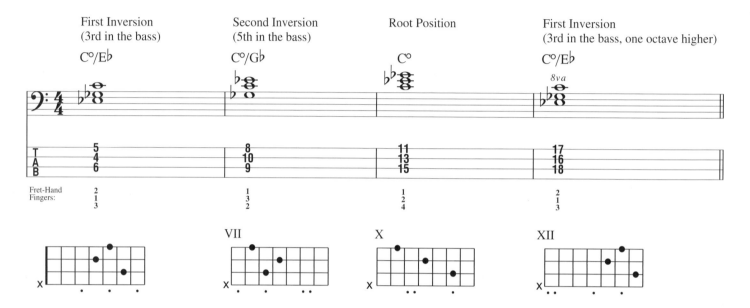

Here are the three different fingerings for the diminished triad in **open** voicings. The first one is very hard to finger when played in this key, but it gets easier in positions up the neck where the frets are closer together.

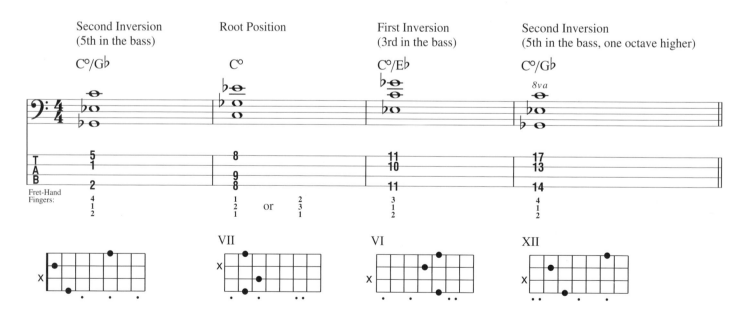

Chapter 5

An augmented triad consists of two major 3rds stacked one on top of the other. Here are the inversions of the augmented triad in **closed** voicings. You will notice they are all the same fingering, just in different positions on the fretboard.

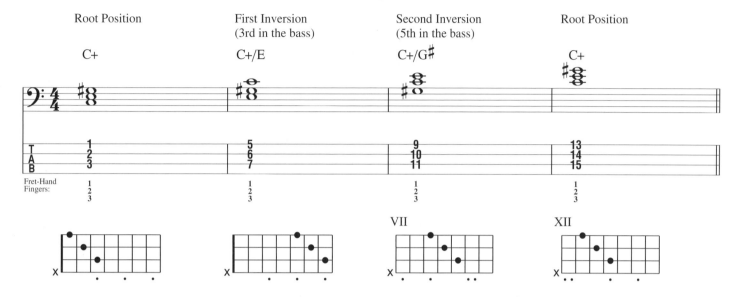

Here are the inversions for the augmented triad in **open** voicings.

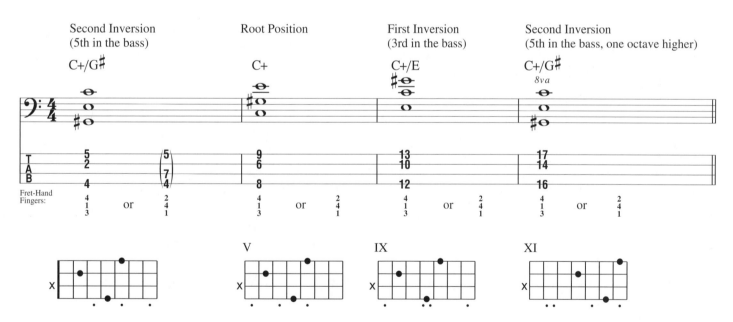

Mixed Triad Exercises

6

Any major key contains seven triads that use scale notes only. To spell these diatonic chords, we began with the 3rd and 5th scale notes over the tonic. The I chord in the key of C was a C major triad built from the C major scale.

To build the II chord, we again use alternating notes from the scale. This time we use scale degrees 2, 4, and 6. In the key of C, the II chord is Dmi.

Continuing the process of building chords from alternating scale notes, we get another minor triad as the III chord from degrees 3, 5, and 7. In C, this chord is Emi.

Continuing the process of building chords, we get major triads on steps 4 and 5, another minor triad on step 6, and finally a diminished triad on step 7.

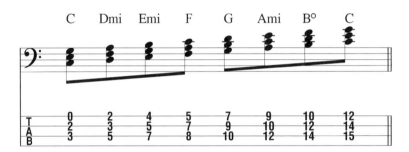

By inverting the triads in the key, we come up with three different harmonic treatments for the C major scale. In these examples, the scale is always found on the top of the chords. Essentially, it's the melody, and we are harmonizing it with chords from the key.

Track 35

First Inversion, Closed Voicing

Track 36

Second Inversion, Closed Voicing

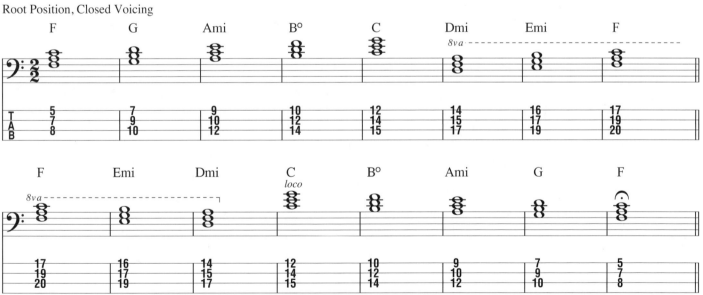

Here is a bass solo supported by chords.

Track 37

Root Position, Closed Voicing

In this example guitar chords come in mainly after the downbeat so they leave room for the bass.

Track 38

Second Inversion, Open Voicing

A Latin piano riff adds some movement to this static bass part.

Track 39

Root Position, Open Voicing

Here is another solo supported with bass chords.

Track 40

First Inversion, Open Voicing

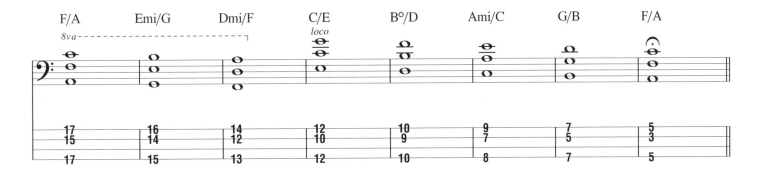

These are open- and closed-voicing *arpeggiated* triads in root position. Arpeggios are chords played one note at a time. Let the notes ring throughout the measure. Here the organ plays a simple melody in the style of "Autumn Leaves."

Here is a similar exercise that incorporates an independent bass line leading chromatically from each chord to the next.

Track 42

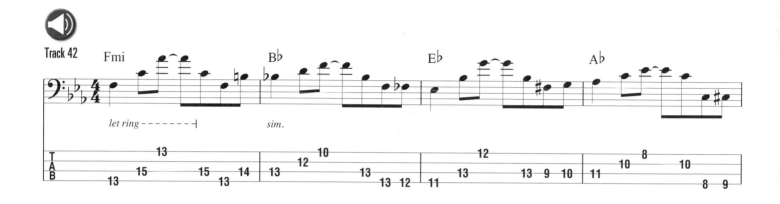

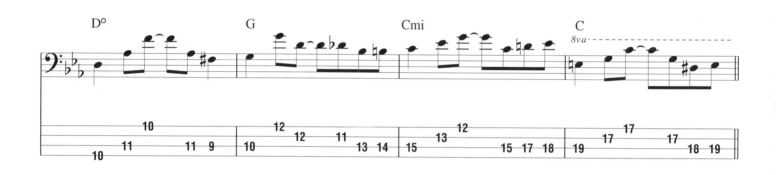

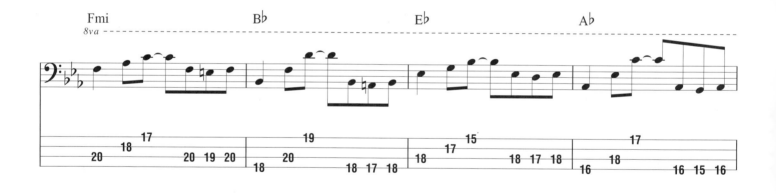

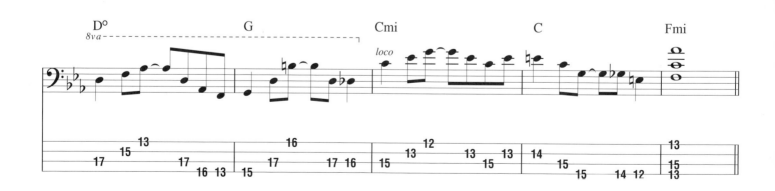

This one alternates between chords and arpeggios, retaining the bass line in a Latin feel.

Here's how you might interpret a chord progression given to you by a singer/songwriter, using arpeggios with some chord punctuations.

Track 44

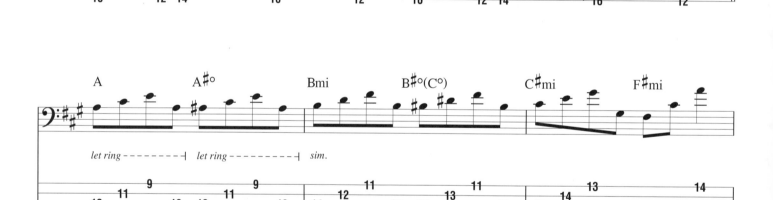

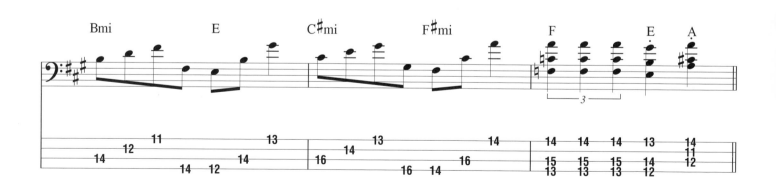

Montuno Pattern

This pattern is built from a simple minor triad. It adds a chromatic descending bass line that goes from the root to the major 6th. It utilizes a twelve-bar minor blues form. The piano adds even more rhythm to this groove with its syncopated pattern.

Track 45

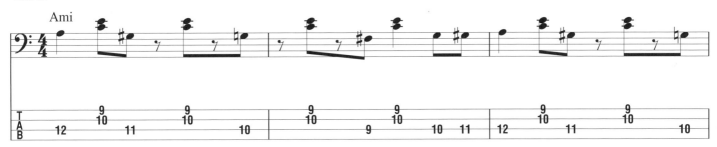

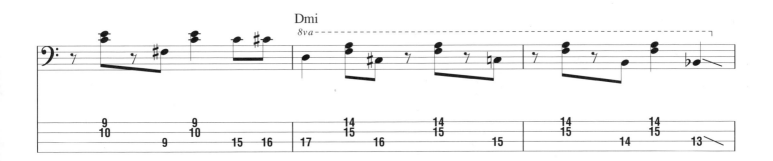

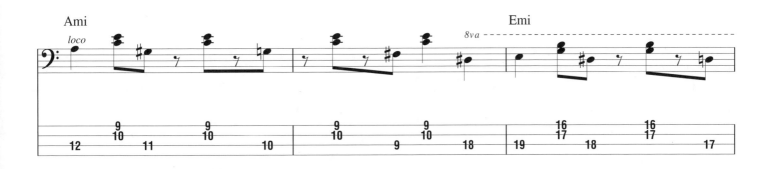

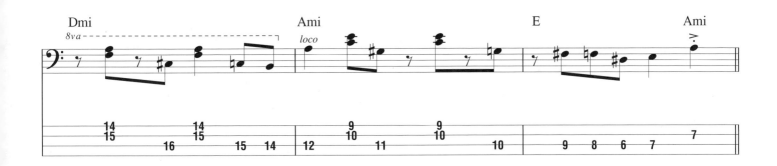

"Greensleeves"

This example uses a melody that has some passing notes. It is not necessary to play a chord on each note. One chord in each measure is enough to outline the harmony of the song. The flute adds a countermelody to the bass.

"Amazing Grace"

This is a great American standard spiritual. An interesting chromatic chord progression in measure 7 connects the root-position C major triad to its first inversion (C/E) in measure 8 by using a II chord (Dm) and then a diminished chord a half step higher.

Track 47

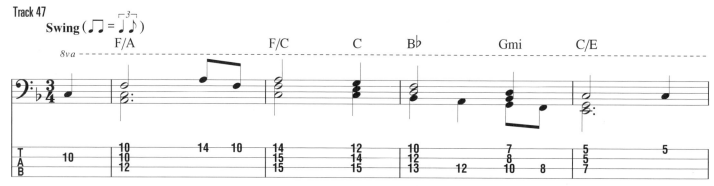

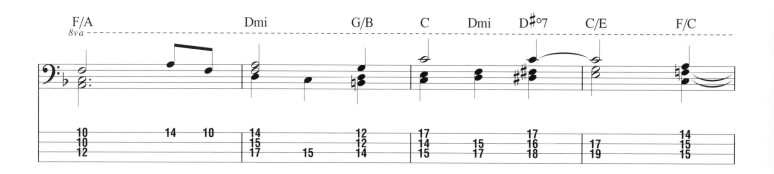

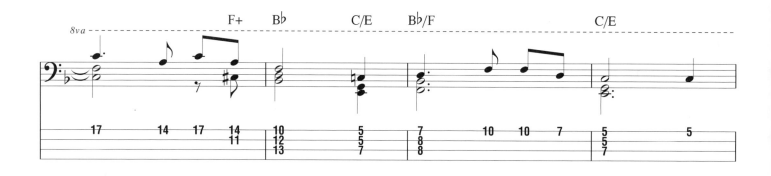

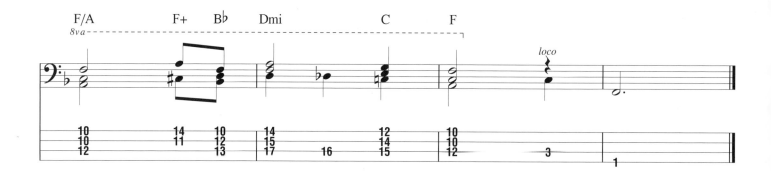

Seventh Chords

7

Seventh chords are four-note chords, the next step up from triads. Seventh chords introduce the possibility of another inversion type: *third inversion*, any chord with its 7th as the lowest note.

The diatonic seventh chords in a major key can be built by stacking 3rds just as we built the diatonic triads. In the key of C, this process of harmonization gives us *major seventh chords* on steps I and IV, *minor seventh chords* on steps II, III, and VI, a *dominant seventh chord* on step V, and a *minor seventh (flat five) chord* on step VII. This figure shows the theoretical locations of the notes in this harmonized scale on the bass—but I can't play it, and I don't expect you to be able to either.

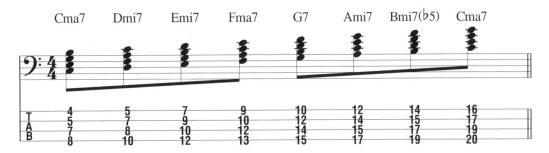

For a cleaner sound on the bass, we will leave one pitch out whenever we have a chord that theoretically includes more than three notes. With open and closed voicings, starting on each possible inversion gives us approximately eight practical ways to play a harmonized scale. I have omitted a few possibilities that don't work.

Closed Voicing 1–3–7
Root Position, 7th on Top, No 5th

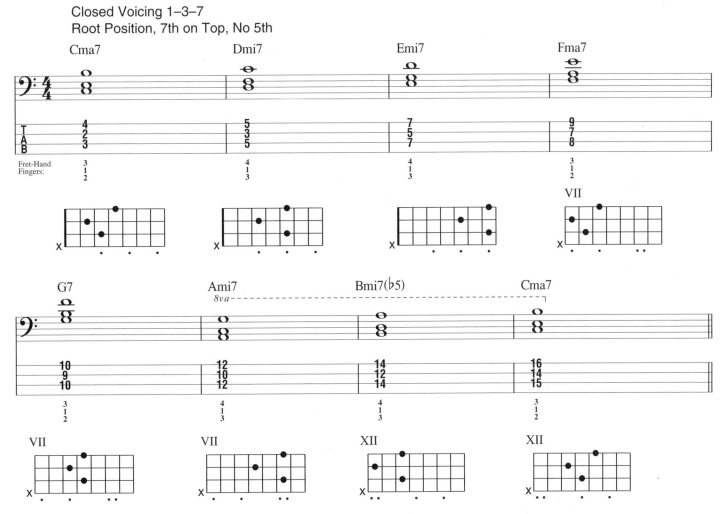

Closed Voicing 1–5–7
Root Position, 7th on Top, No 3rd

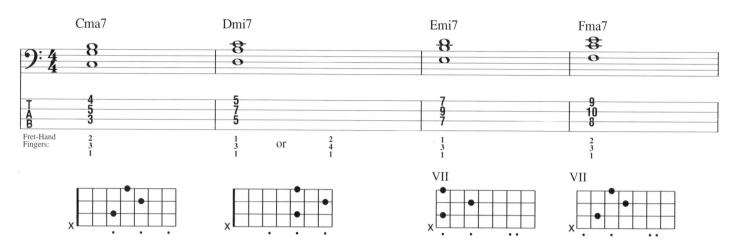

Closed Voicing 3–7–1
First Inversion, Root on Top, No 5th

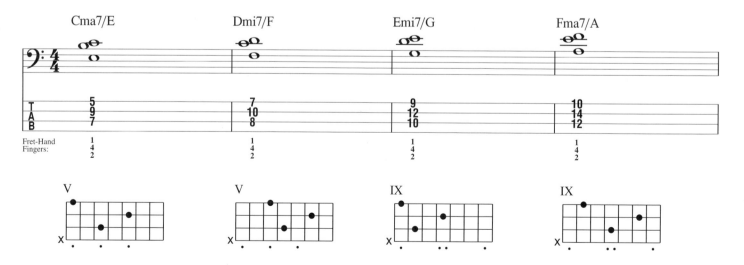

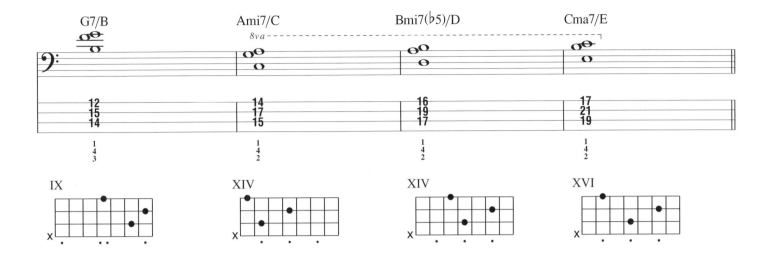

Closed Voicing 5–7–3
Second Inversion, 3rd on Top, No Root
With the root missing, these chords can also be looked at as triads a diatonic 3rd higher.

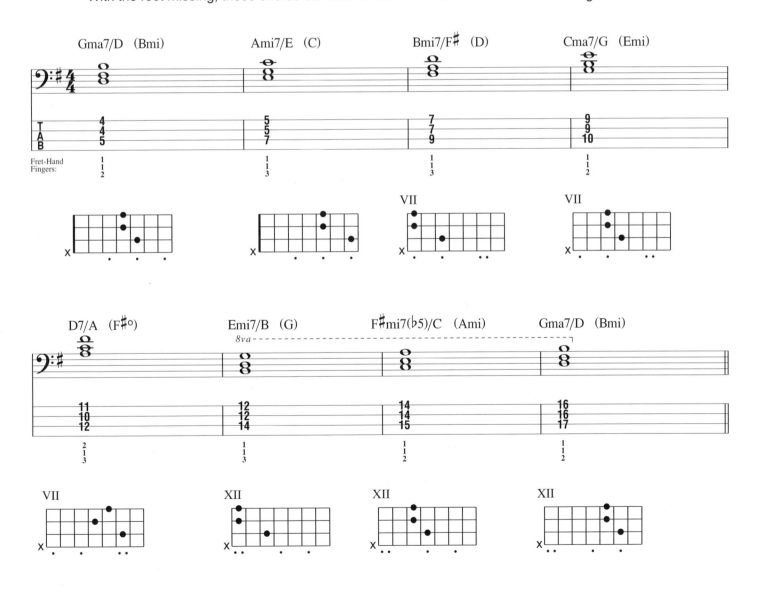

Closed Voicing 7–3–5
Third Inversion, 5th on Top, No Root
Note the equivalent triads (as mentioned in the previous example).

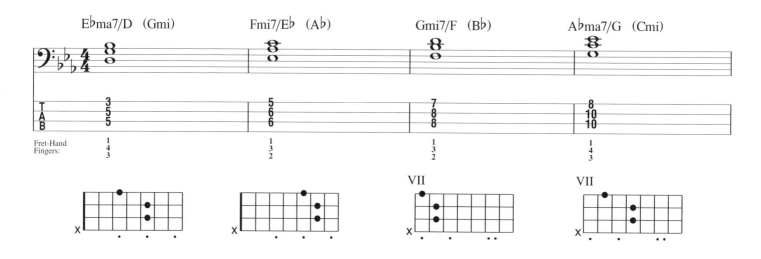

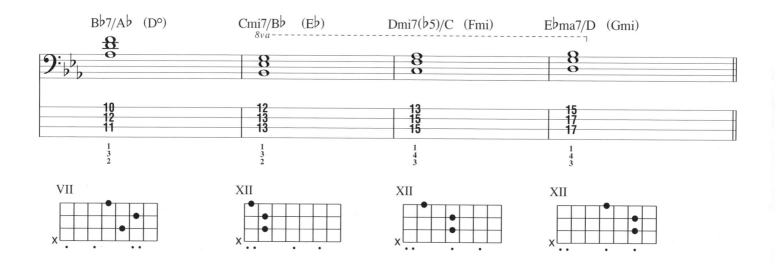

Open Voicing 1–7–3
Root Position, 3rd on Top, No 5th

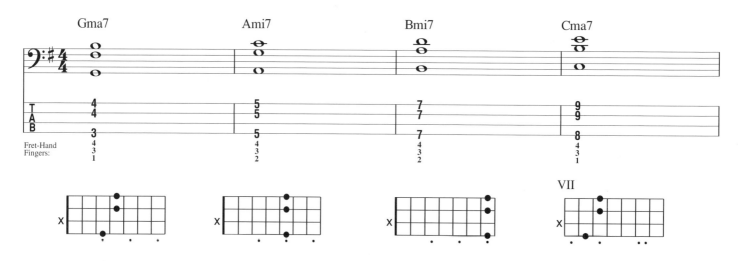

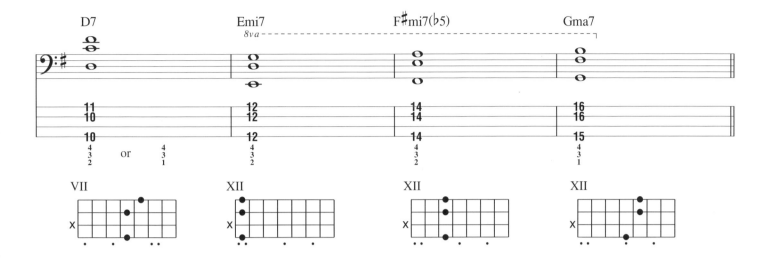

Open Voicing 1–7–5
Root Position, 5th on Top, No 3rd

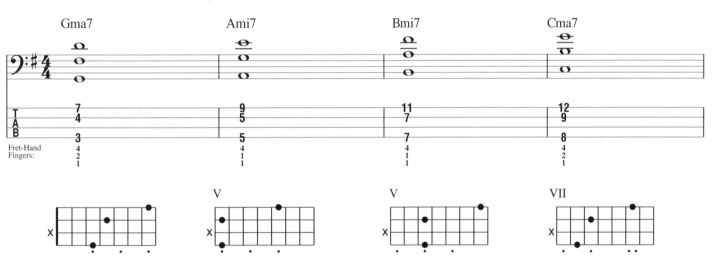

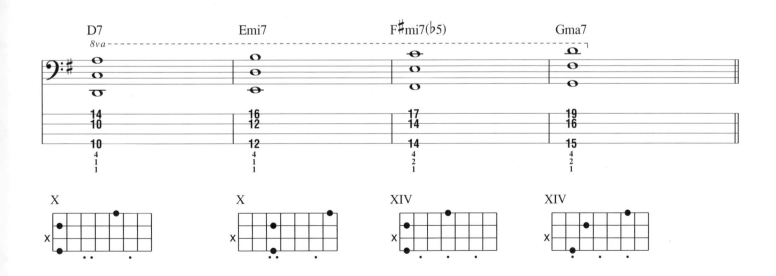

Open Voicing 1–5–7–3
Root Position, 3rd on Top
This voicing sounds very thick and is not recommended for frequent use.

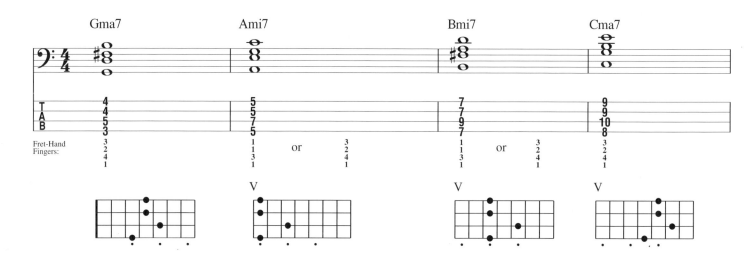

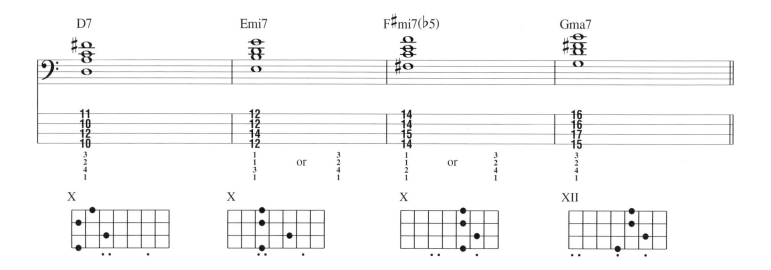

Seventh Chord Exercises

8

Chord Progression in C

This common progression appears in the jazz standard "Autumn Leaves."

Track 48

Track 49

Chord Progression in B♭

Here is another common jazz progression.

8

In the next three examples the additional instruments play melodies and solo on top of the bass chords.

Arpeggiated Chord Progression in G

This progression originated from the standard "I Got Rhythm."

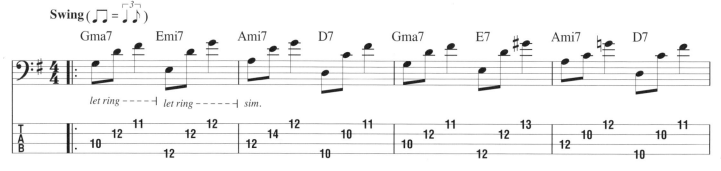

Track 50

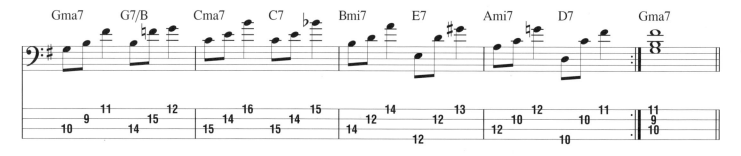

Broken Chord Progression in F

Try this accompaniment in the style of "The Girl from Ipanema."

Track 51

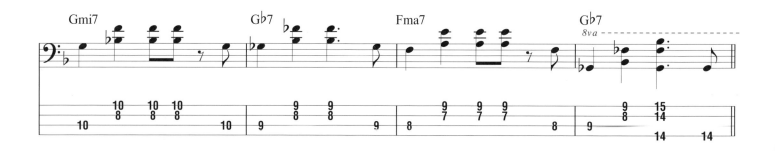

52

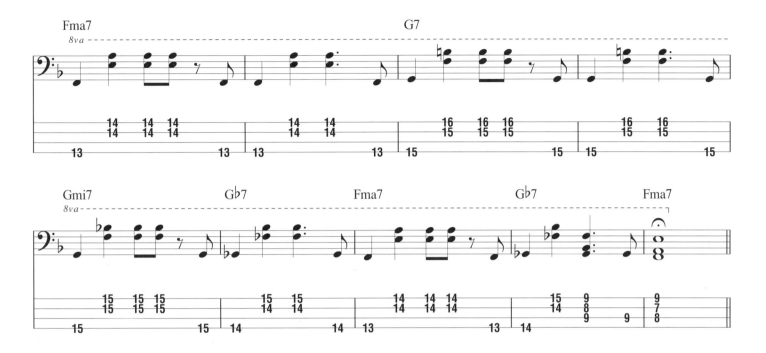

Jazz Blues in F

Track 52

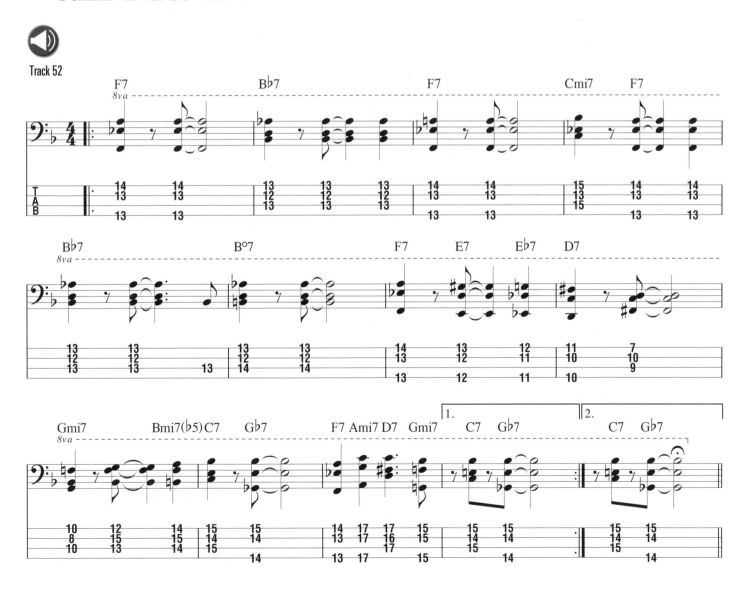

"When the Saints Go Marching In"

This is a favorite American spiritual. A funky guitar lick makes it groove even more.

Track 53

"Go Tell It on the Mountain"

Here the guitar reinforces the backbeats.

Track 54

Swing (♪♪ = ♪³♪)

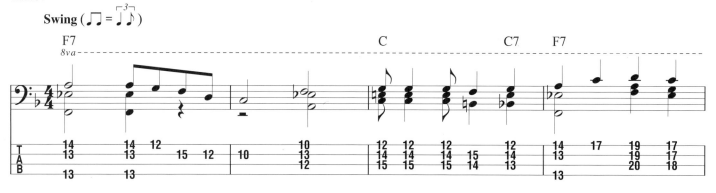

Chapter 8

55

"Looking Back"
by Dominik Hauser

Track 55

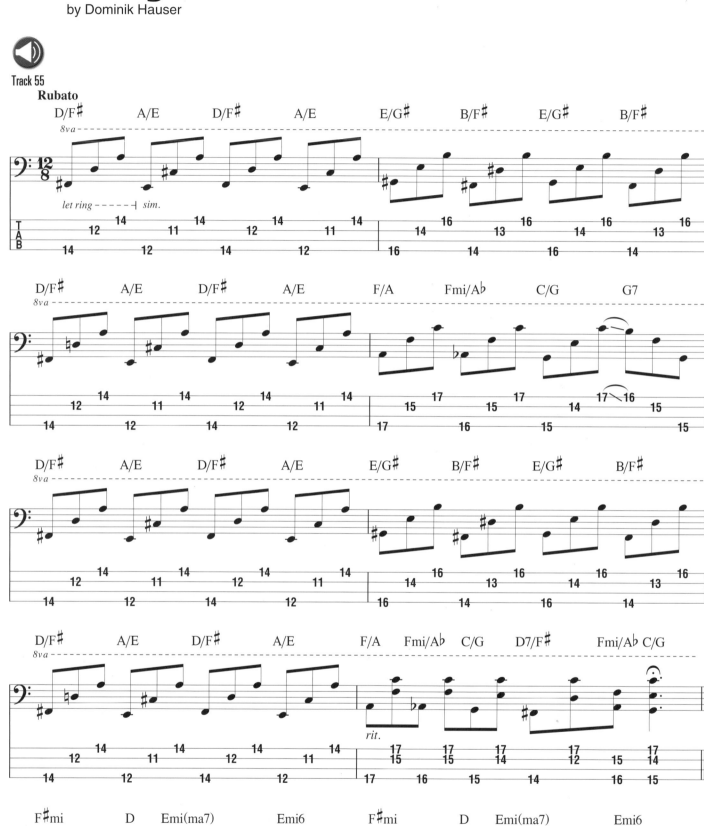

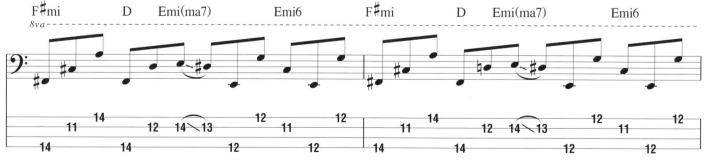

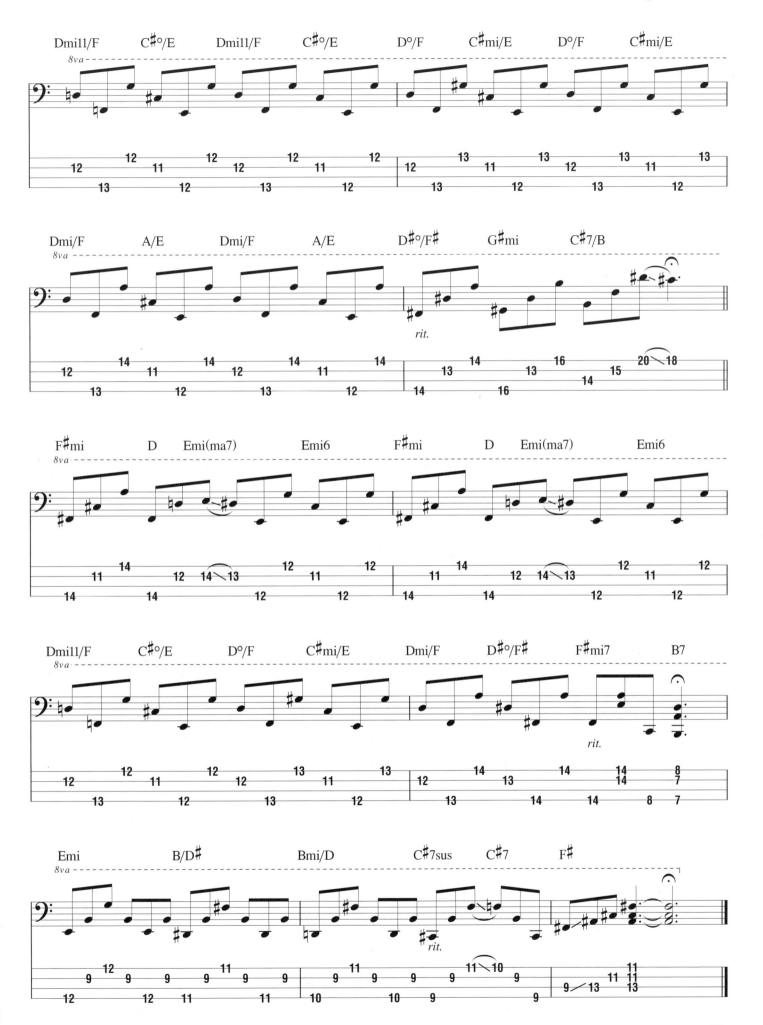

Playing Chords with a Bass Line

9

In these examples, use only your thumb for the bass line. The index, middle, and ring fingers should be used to play the two- or three-note chord voicings.

I–IV–I–IV–V in C

Here the bass plays an independent Motown-type line, while the chords outline the 3rds and 5ths. The acoustic guitar adds more of a folky feel to the groove.

Track 56

I–VI–I–II–V in D

This track shows how you can play roots and 5ths interspersed with chords. Chromatic passing notes connect to the roots in measures 1 and 3. The guitar plays harmonics, adding a nice texture.

Track 57

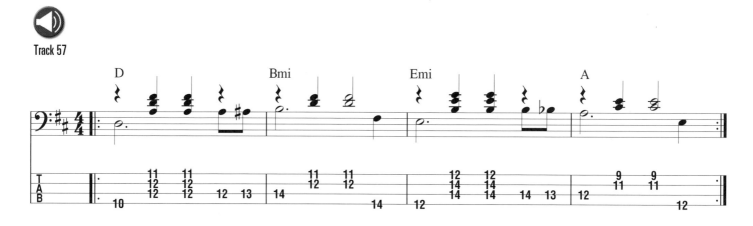

II–V–I in C

Again the bass line plays the roots and the 5ths, while the chords play 3rds and 7ths. The guitar reinforces the chords by playing them on beat three.

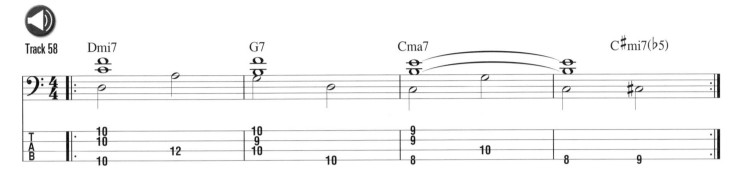

This is the same as the previous example, in a higher position. Now the guitar plays extended chords on beat two, so it won't get in the way of the bass.

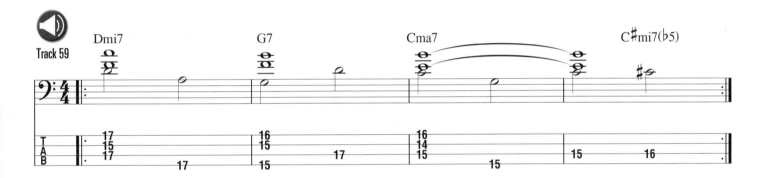

II–V–I–IV in B♭

The bass line plays the roots and the 5ths, while the chords play 3rds and 7ths.

Here's the same progression in a higher position.

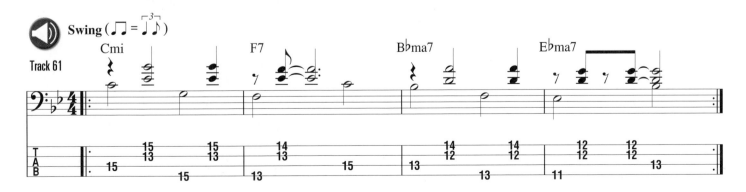

Rock Groove in Fmi

The guitar enforces the progression with distorted accented chords.

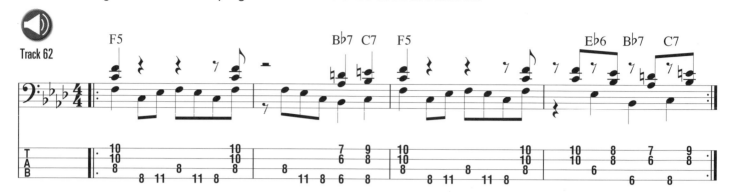

Gospel Groove in G

This works over dominant seventh chords or major triads.

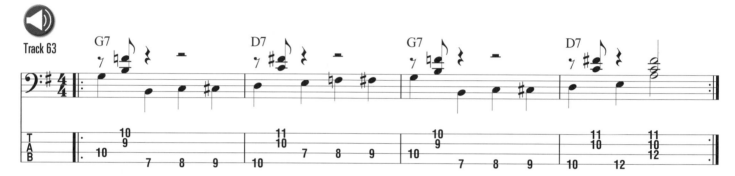

Walking Bass Line with 3rd and 7th Chord Fragments

This accompaniment is used frequently in a jazz trio setting to support a guitarist with harmonies. It is a different interpretation of the progression on track 48. This very common progression is a II–V–I–IV in F, followed by II–V–I in D minor. The D7 in measure 8 is a non-diatonic chord (the V of II) that leads us back to the Gm7 (II) at the beginning.

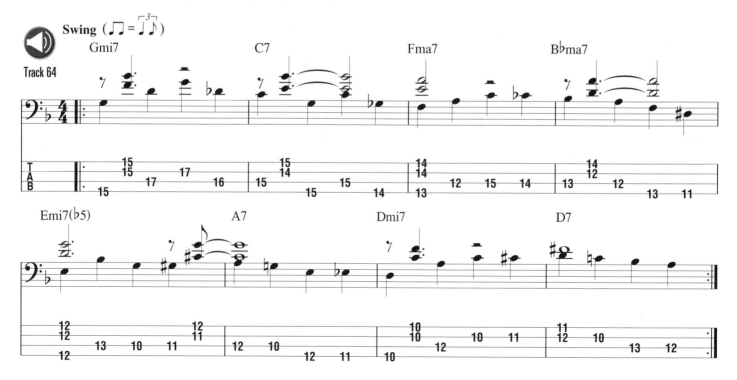

Here is the same progression as before, in the key of B♭ major. Practice it in different keys. This is how you could *comp* (accompany) on a jazz tune while the guitar is taking a solo.

Track 65

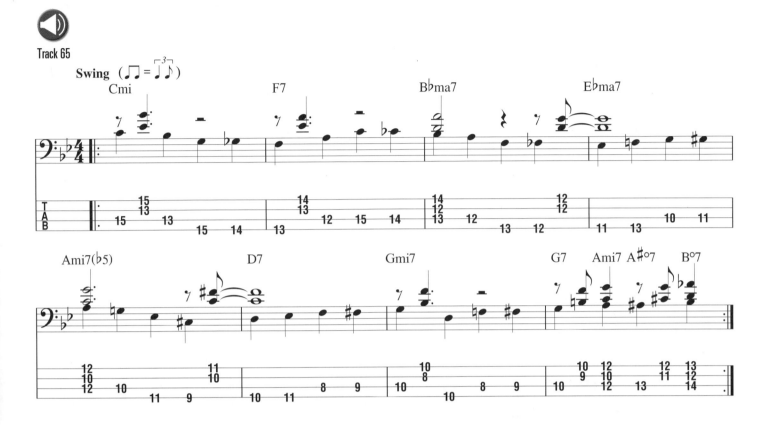

Here is a similar approach, this time in C minor, with a bossa nova feel. Notice the repeating bass line/chord pattern. This is how you could comp on a Latin tune while the guitar is taking a solo.

Track 66

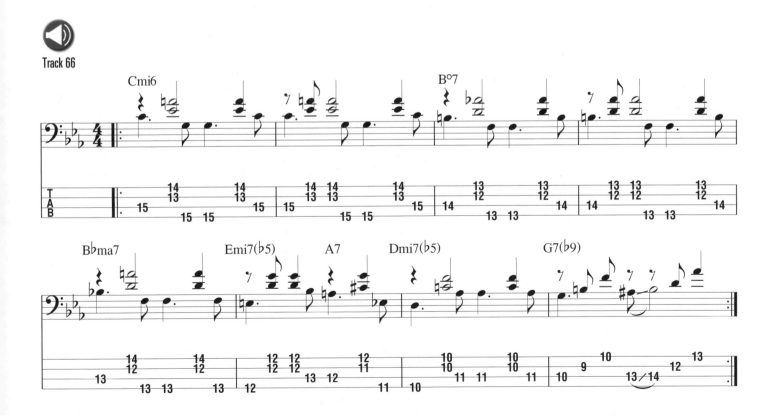

Funk Rock Pattern with Passing Chords

Track 67

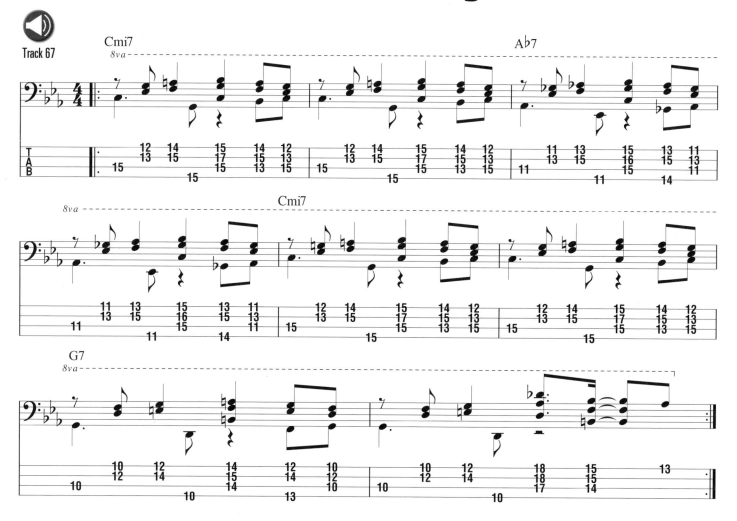

Funk Rock Patterns over B♭ Blues Progression

This is in the style of "Watermelon Man." Chromatic passing chords lead to each change. The funky guitar really adds to this groove.

Track 68

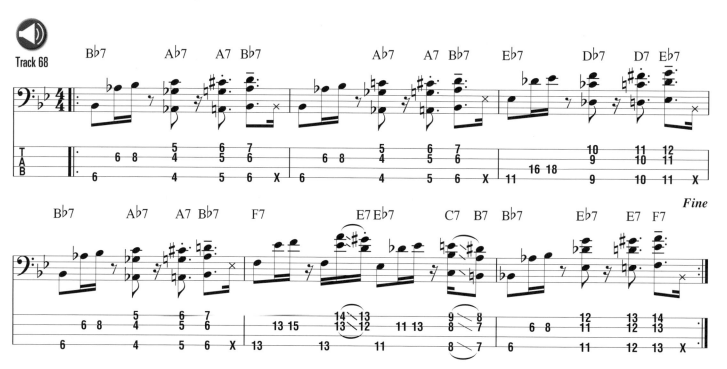

Using Chords in Different Styles

10

Here are some patterns to give you an idea of how you can incorporate chords into a bass part in various styles. It is useful to analyze and emulate the parts played by the guitar or keyboard in a given style. I also encourage you to do what I did: try anything, see if it works, and have fun.

Heavy Metal

The chords are mainly power chords—roots and 5ths. Play this with distortion and a pick. Playing like a guitarist using all downstrokes of the pick gives the desired jackhammer-like precision. On the repeat the guitar adds a solo.

Track 69

Grunge

Here are more beefy downstroke-picked power chords with distortion. On the repeat the guitar strengthens the chords by doubling them an octave higher than the bass.

Track 70

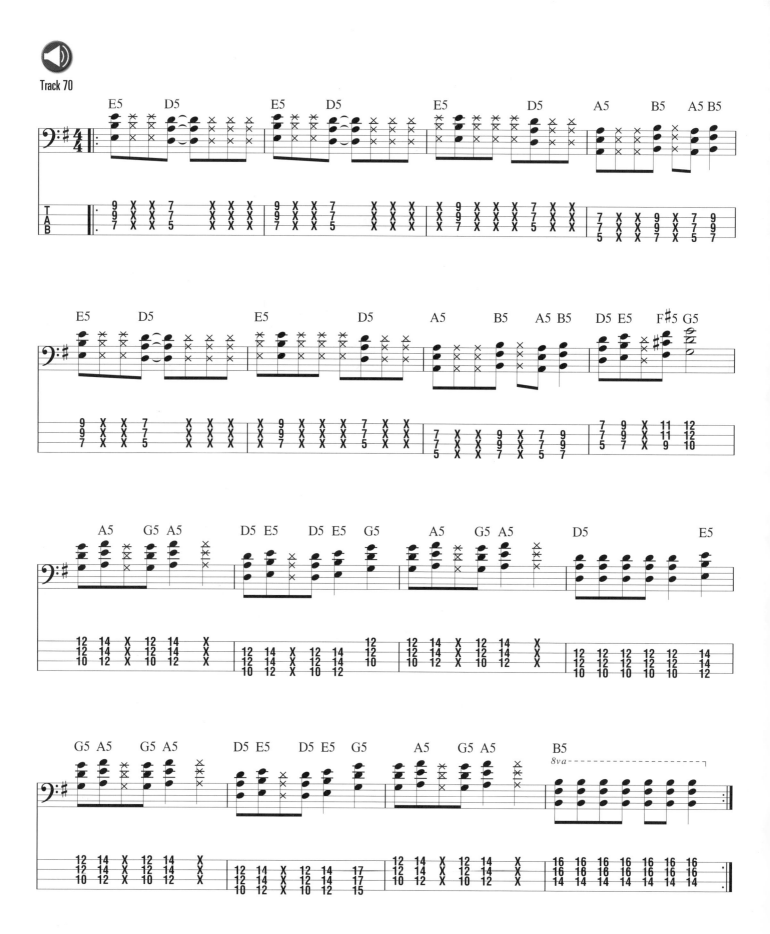

Funk

This heavily-syncopated example follows a B♭ blues progression using all dominant seventh chords. The guitar plays a muted single-string line to add another layer of interest.

Track 71

Funk Rock

This was played with only the pick using down and upstrokes. It's very similar to how a guitarist would comp a funk tune. The high guitar riff adds balance to the lower bass chords.

Track 72

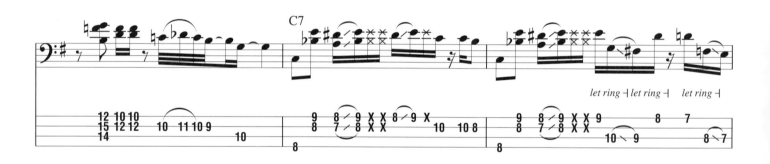

Jazz

Notice the lack of a definite pattern in the chord punctuations. This is a requirement of the bebop jazz style. 9ths and ♯11ths but very few roots are used. Here the piano outlines the roots and the guitar plays a melody on the repeat.

Track 73

Here is another jazz progression; this time in D minor. This particular progression is played very open; the timekeeping aspect of the part is sparse.

Track 74

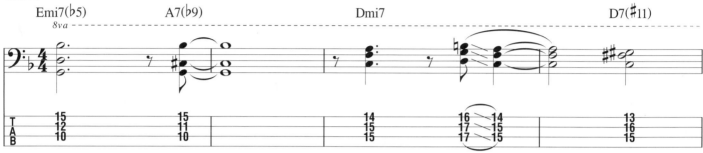

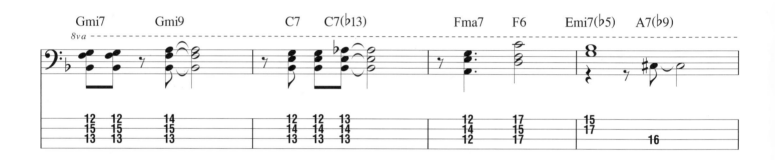

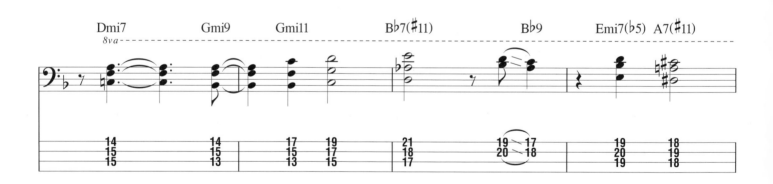

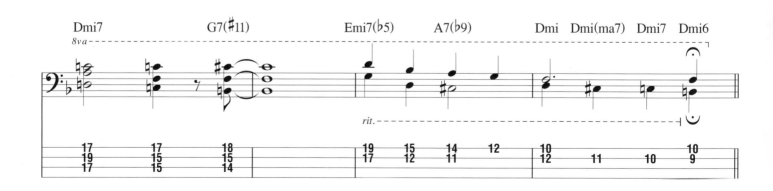

Bossa Nova

Notice the repetitive rhythm. Mainly 3rds and 7ths are used, with a few 5ths and higher extensions (9ths, 11ths, ♭13ths). Again the guitar plays a muted single-string line for contrast.

Track 75

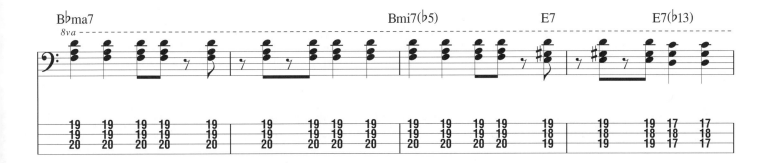

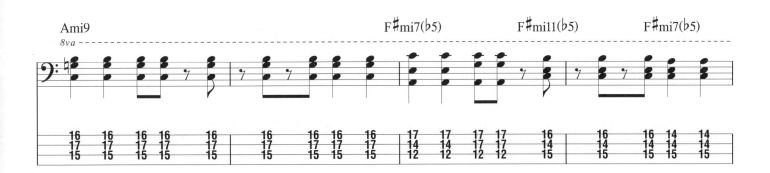

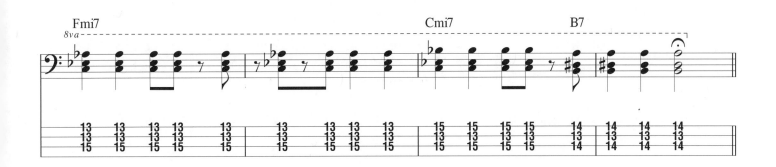

Rock 'n' Roll

This is a common guitar pattern based in the blues. While the bass holds down the chords the guitar has the freedom to solo.

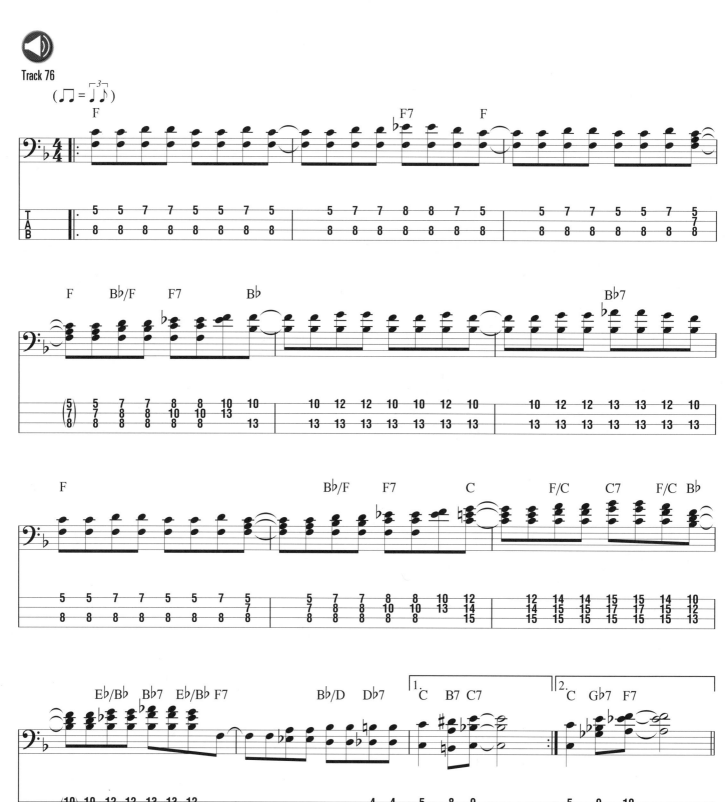

Track 76

Chord Glossary

These are all practical chord voicings for the bass. There are many more possibilities, but these are the most common and useful. Rather than trying to memorize them all as fingering shapes, it's better to study which notes are needed to fulfill the formula implied by the name. All notes are compared to the major scale. For example, a major triad uses 1, 3, and 5 from the major scale. In a minor triad the 3rd is minor when compared to the major scale; the 5th is unchanged.

You will notice that some voicings can be used for more than one chord, with a different note being thought of as the root. That is because we don't always play every note of the chord. After the chord descriptions you will find their most common symbols. In general you will find that closed voicings sound more clear. I added an asterisk next to my favorites.

TRIADS

Major Triad: 1–3–5
C, C△, Cma, CMA, Cmaj, Cma, Cmaj

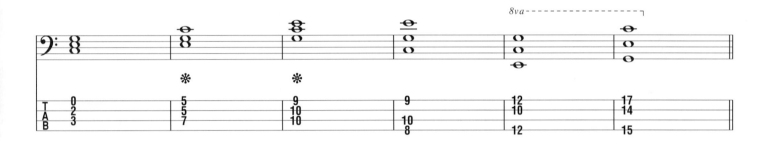

Minor Triad: 1–♭3–5
Cm, C-, Cmi, CMI, c

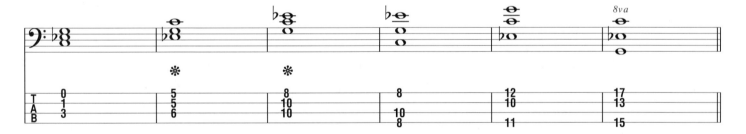

Diminished Triad: 1–♭3–♭5
C°, Cdim

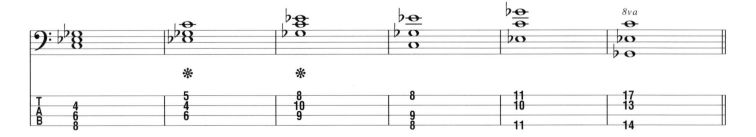

Augmented Triad: 1–3–♯5

C+, Caug, CAug

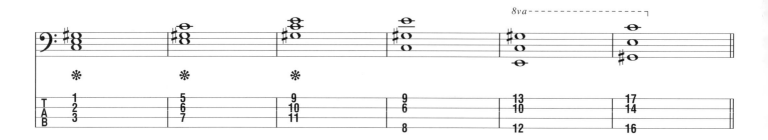

SIXTH CHORDS

Major Sixth: 1–3–5–6

C6, Cma6, CMA6, C^ma6

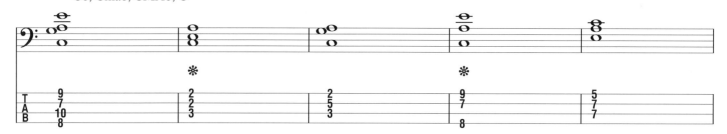

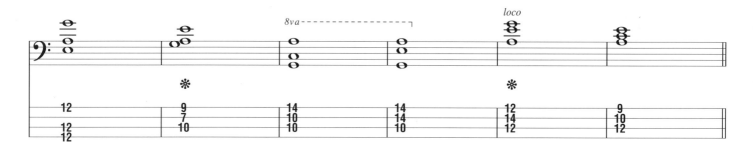

Minor Sixth: 1–♭3–5–6 (only the 3rd is minor)

Cm6, C-6, Cmi6, CMI6

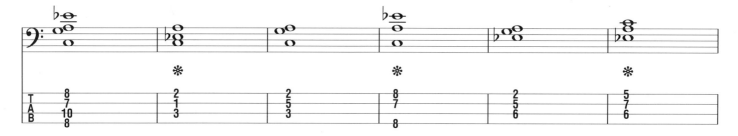

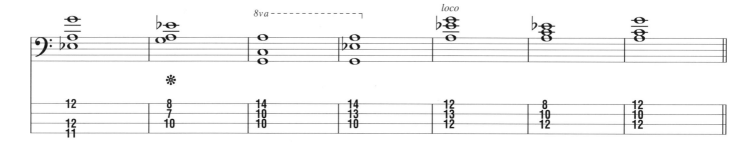

SEVENTH CHORDS

Major Seventh: 1–3–5–7
Cma7, C△7, CMA7, Cmaj7, Cj7

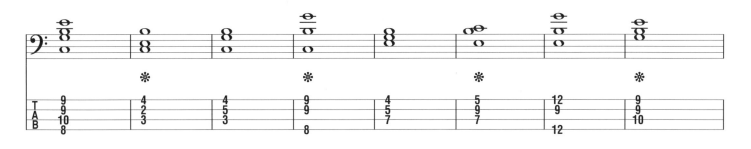

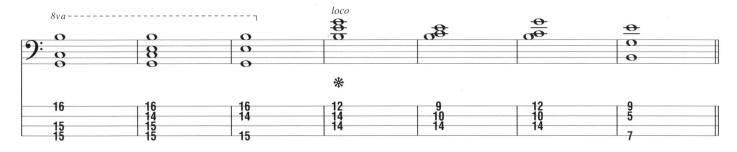

Dominant Seventh: 1–3–5–♭7
C7

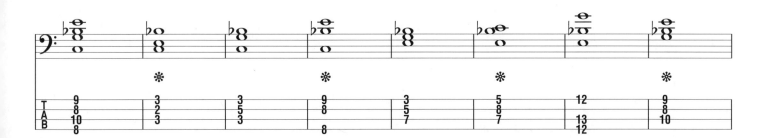

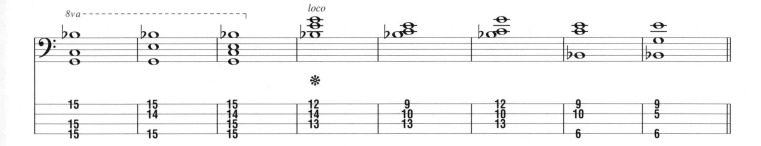

Minor Seventh: 1–♭3–5–♭7
Cmi7, C-7, CMI7, Cm7

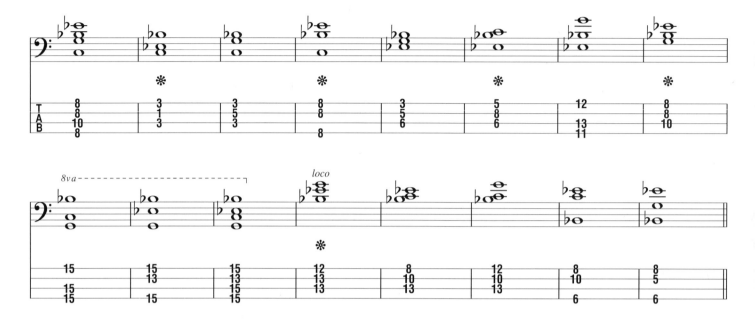

Minor Seventh Flat Five: 1–♭3–♭5–♭7
Cmi7(♭5), CMI7♭5, Cm7♭5, C⌀7, C-7♭5

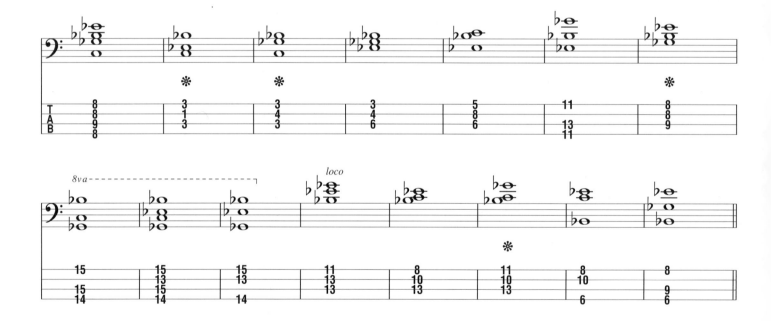

Diminished Seventh: 1–♭3–♭5–♭♭7

C°7, Cdim7

This chord is built by stacking a series of minor 3rd intervals. This symmetrical construction can be moved in minor 3rds, resulting in essentially the same chord.

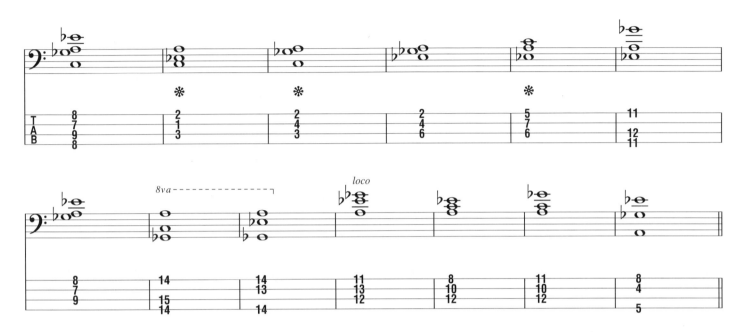

Minor Major Seventh: 1–♭3–5–7

Cm(maj7), Cmi^{ma7}, C-^Δ7, CMIma7, Cm^{ma7}, Cmi^Δ7

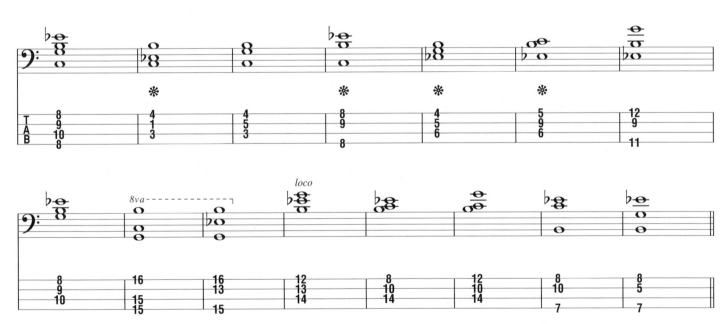

EXTENDED CHORDS

Major Add Ninth: 1–3–5–9
Cma(add 9), Cmaj(add9), CMA(add9), C△add9

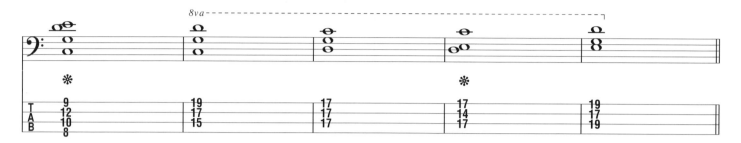

Minor Add Ninth: 1–♭3–5–9
Cmi(add 9), C-(add9), Cm(add9)

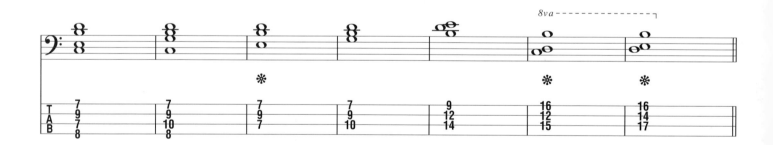

Major Ninth: 1–3–5–7–9
Cma9, Cmaj7(9), C△9, CMA9

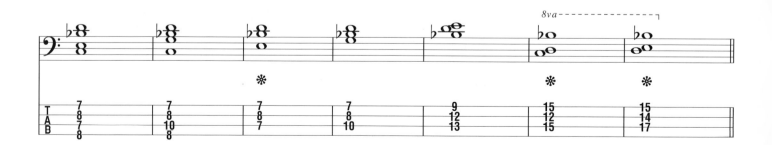

Dominant Ninth: 1–3–5–♭7–9
C9, C7(9)

Minor Ninth: 1–♭3–5–♭7–9
Cmi9, Cm9, Cm7(9), C-9

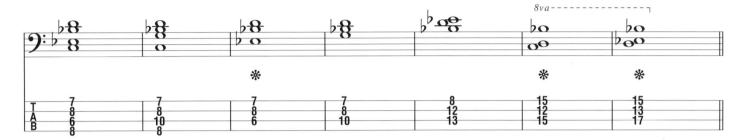

Minor Eleventh: 1–♭3–5–♭7–11
Cm11, Cmi7(11), CMI7(11)

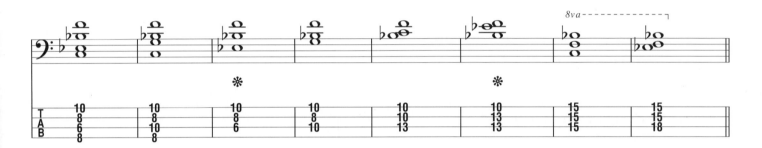

Major Thirteenth: 1–3–5–7–13
Cma13, Cmaj7(13)

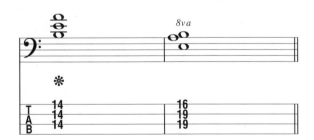

Dominant Seventh Suspended Fourth: 1–4–5–♭7
C7sus, C7sus4

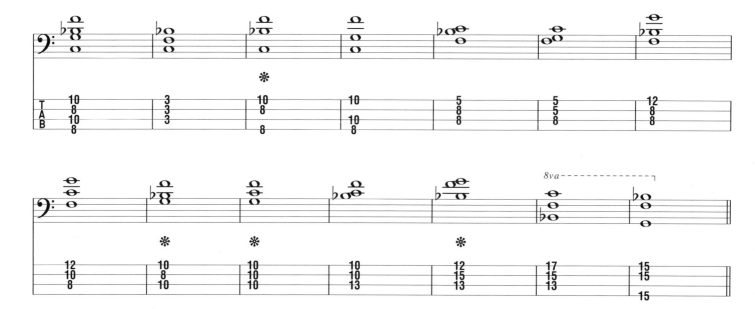

Dominant Thirteenth: 1–3–5–♭7–13
C13, C7(13)

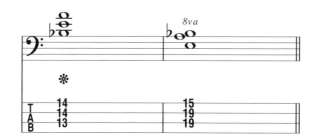

ALTERED CHORDS

Major Seventh Sharp Five: 1–3–♯5–7
Cma7(♯5), C△7♯5, Cma7♯5, CMA7+5, Cmaj7+5, Cj7+5

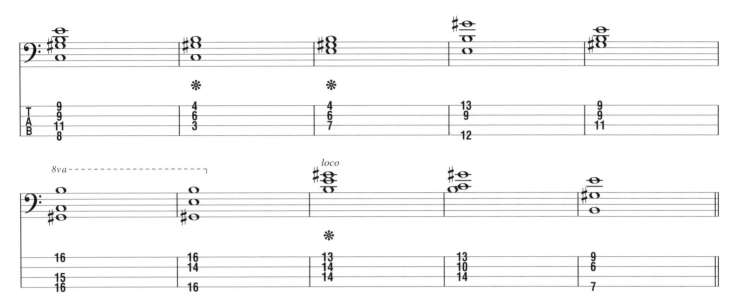

Major Seventh Sharp Eleventh: 1–3–5–7–♯11
Cma7(♯11), CMA+11, C△♯11, C△+11

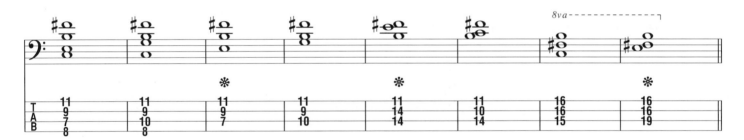

Dominant Seventh Sharp Five: 1–3–♯5–♭7
C7(♯5), C+7

This is the same chord as the dominant seventh flat thirteenth: C7(♭13), C7-13

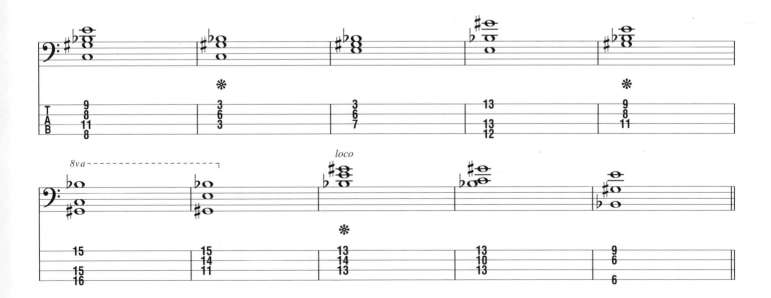

Dominant Seventh Flat Five: 1–3–♭5–♭7
C7(♭5), C7-5

This is the same chord as the dominant seventh sharp eleventh: C7♯11, C7+11

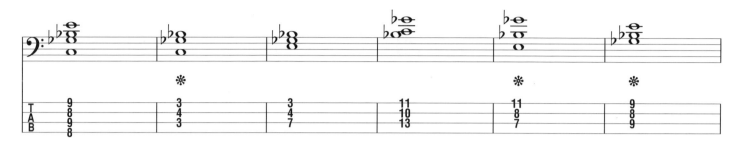

Dominant Seventh Flat Ninth: 1–3–5–♭7–♭9
C7(♭9)

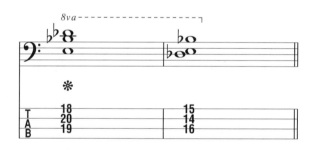

Dominant Seventh Sharp Ninth: 1–3–5–♭7–♯9
C7(♯9)

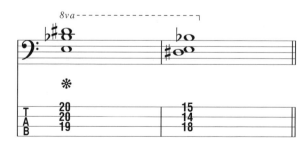